MYSTERIOUS CHA

SHREYAS GHADGE

Published by Publishing Expert
Hanumangarh Road Near Naveen Sethi Hospital Under
Flyover, Punjab Abohar -152116
publishingexpert.org@gmail.com

© **Shreyas Ghadge**

Design(s) Publishing Expert

" **Mysterious Changes In Life**"

By : Shreyas Ghadge

ISBN -13: 9789392001130
ISBN -10: 9392001130

Cover Design : Publishing Expert

Price : 249.00 INR

Printed & Typeset by : Publishing Expert

ABOUT THE BOOK

If there is one thing in this world, it is the personality, the courage, and the dream.   It is said that life is meaningless unless you make your dreams come true by creating some kind of stress in life. Just as there is a moment in our lives when there is no salt in our food. But if a person does not fulfill his own dream, he will not be recognized for it. It is easy to be a cricketer with a bat in one's hand, but it is just as difficult to enter the battlefield and be a great player in front of the world. And the world wants your result, not your hard work. As long as you do not present the proof of your dreams to the world, it cannot be said to be fulfilled. And the day you are satisfied with your mind, you will realize your dreams come true. The dream has been fulfilled in front of everyone since childhood. And a new subject of my life, a new chapter has started through a writer. When your dream is big, you are not alone. But give your dream for a while in your life and try to follow it diligently

ABOUT THE AUTHOR

My name is Shreyas Ghadge. I am 22 years old and I am a civil engineering student who has just graduated from YCCE College of Engineering. In fact, there are many things in life that we have never seen, and if we have seen, we have never been able to put them into words. But I am a person who has looked at a lot of things carefully. This is the second book of my life. It is my sincere desire to reach out to the people through this book. Just like I am a student of civil engineering, there are some threads in my life that have to be tied to something, which has been expressed in words from time to time with the help of specific knots. Changes in the whole approach are presented through this book.

CONTENTS

Chapter -1 Change

"Change" Every moment is a time for man to change himself. Because basically he needs it to make them mature. And not just for the sake of getting ahead in life, but for a lot of personal things, he has to change himself. Some changes he has to take on himself because of people. So he has to make some changes himself. But in this vast world, he is not sure that he will understand everything. He has to understand many things. And from the movement he has today, he knows the purpose of tomorrow. Not everything will be according to man's taste. There are some things that need to be changed to make it a hobby. The amount of change is decreasing day by day, the root cause of which is that the inclusion of many specific elements in human beings is increasing on a large scale. Such things as arrogance, hatred, anger are becoming more and more prevalent. He did not want to make any changes in his life, even though he had suffered from it many times before. Because behind it, there is a world called pride in his life, he is mingling in it for hours. Which means it's about to be the most delusional time of the year, as well. Often a person loses his life because of such changes. And no matter who tells him these changes, nothing will happen until he himself tries to bring about these changes in us or he doesn't think that these changes are going to be very important in our lives. And that is the law of creation, you will do your work, you will get your reward according to your deeds. And who doesn't make mistakes? After all, if you are a human being, it is not wrong to make mistakes. If they are wrong, then we do not understand the mistakes and change them. Because a person who does not make mistakes will not experience it, and if he does not experience it, he will not be able to move forward. And failure is not far from some life, it is like a tool of our success, in which we can achieve success by making the necessary changes and converting those tools into tools.

Age is not required to bring about change. All that is needed is your understanding of your feelings. If your special understanding is like that of an understanding person, you can easily make the positive change you want. But if you are living in the company of fools, then it is just as difficult for you to change that. It is said that the basic human nature never goes away, just as "the tail of a dog is crooked". She can never be straight. But if we think and believe in the mind, we can change it a little bit and treat it properly. For example, if a person has a passionate nature, it does not mean that he is passionate as usual. And yet love can conquer the whole world. So man should never stop loving. Love is often the key to helping them change things for the better. There are some changes that we can only try to bring about but they are basically ready to bring about change so somewhere they are shown as wasting our hard work. The root cause is "money". In the current situation, the poison called money has also increased to create a distinct identity among the four people in the House. Naturally, these people have a different kind of pride in the rain. So no matter how much you treat them, if you treat them with love, they will misinterpret them and persecute your feelings. Basically, a person who is proud of his money needs to change himself, he needs to be humble so that he doesn't have to worry about anything tomorrow. But as long as money is with man, he is not ready to constantly change. And since it hurts the humble person, he often needs to change. This is going to happen automatically the day he realizes the change. But one of the biggest unforgettable beauties of human life is that a self-respecting person should never give up. This is how things happen at home, because the situation in life takes a turn for the worse. But there is a purpose to giving up self-esteem. The price of 4 people value you only when you hold on to your self-esteem. Over time, if you let go of your self-esteem in front of everyone, your value will surely seem to disappear somewhere. And this is the biggest change. If it always motivates you to assimilate. In fact, man's park is always difficult and in times of crisis. There is no one who can tell the difference between a person running for help and someone who is leaning on help. Until then you have to understand and the person who really came to the rescue is definitely no less for you then. When the person whom we trust the most goes well without running for help, we know his judgment and according to his nature we know his true purpose, so we make a change in his nature about his mind. It makes you very uncomfortable about going well but if that discomfort happens today it will help you to live easily tomorrow. There are two facts behind everything. Now that person is fearless about how he looks at things. It is said that when a person is angry, the things he says in anger are literally out of his mind and they are also true. But another fact related to this is that when a person speaks in anger, he is not conscious, but once the anger is gone, he has nothing in his mind. Both of these events are dealt with in the right way and with the right approach. But with these two things in mind, the person changes himself and creates a different feeling about the person in front of him. It is not yet clear which of these feelings is right. But the rest is about man making mistakes, but no one in this world is right, every person is the same, time forces man to take shape accordingly. In fact, if you try to change yourself by making mistakes in every person, you will have to make changes every day because making mistakes will take you less than half your life.

Every time a person has to face something, from one point of view or another, one thing always happens to him is change. We all understand this. But change is not only made from one point of view, but also from another unspeakable, that is, from a mysterious change, a strange change. But there are many reasons to recognize the strange change. Man has a different identity, his point of view, which lays many traps to shape different perspectives to see that strange change. For example, when a given person earns his success by hard work, there can be two kinds of change in him, one of which is that unity can make him proud, or motivate him to face people. When a person is working under someone's hand, then when he decides to build his own empire, there are two kinds of changes that can be called bizarre changes, either he thinks of himself as master and teaches his servants proper work according to his experience, otherwise While working, he can continue to make himself a porter. It depends on the style of thinking a person has to accept anything.

It is said that one should not be inferior to anything in life. Because nothing ever fails, it just hints at a lesson in your life to teach you and tell you something. You need more than luck to succeed in affiliate business. Not only that, but there are some changes that we do not fully agree with. But if the mind is explained, the consequences are extremely beneficial. But one of the important changes is the definite decision. There are also two types of definite change. Sometimes it leads us to a very good path, sometimes it leads to a very painful and repentant path. For example, when we make a definite decision to move forward in our career, sometimes the benefit is so great that we have a certain kind of pride in ourselves. But certain decisions, as they relate to your relationship, often lead to deep remorse. One thing to always keep in mind is that everyone experiences it, even when we are going through a very angry mood. So you need to be very careful about your words. When arguing, sir, we try to break the relationship with the help of a definite decision. So somewhere your mind gets a kind of relief. But when it comes to the future, there is often a great deal of remorse for that. And there are always reasons to be upset because of this definite decision of yours.

Another important factor in the mysterious change is the dangerous change.

Why not? This is a typical sign of change. Like for example we make a lot of decisions for the satisfaction of any small thing. Because some decisions are very important, change never happens except as it should. But change is dangerous when a person with a negative attitude makes a decision that he will regret for the rest of his life. Most people make this mysterious change when they are very angry, and even pull themselves out of stress. But if anyone has experienced a thing, they will know that there is no such thing as perfection in this world. Even so, owning one is still beyond the reach of the average person.

Chapter –2- Emotion

The vast majority of people who make hasty decisions, of course, do so out of a lack of emotion. In fact, we cannot identify the nature of a person, but the nature of that person is made up of different perspectives. That is because of the way the person views the world. Some people understand things so well that their nature helps them to make decisions accordingly. For that, man has to be chant every time, and in today's world of deception, there is no choice but to make chant. It does not require any age or your personality. Humanity accepts understanding as it should be. But in the basic element of each person, emotion addresses his personality. Simply put, when it comes time to help a person, he decides to help according to his feelings. No matter how much one tries to hide one's feelings and temperament, it is not hidden. One study found that a person who tries to make a decision based on emotion is not at all 100% right.

People love through emotion, people help through emotion. It sounds so sweet. But the dangerous decisions in life are also made by the deception of the people by the feeling that the person in front has misused with most of the people. He has often learned a lot from these mistakes, but he has often been shameless and deceives people today with the help of those feelings. The people of today are very fraternal. By the way people express their grief by giving contextual explanations in front of people, the person in front goes deep somewhere. Often those things are also true but from the depths of it, when a person helps them, they harm themselves by helping with a strong attitude. In fact, in addition to learning man, one must also learn to recognize man. This is the mistake of naive people. Reminds people at work and forgets immediately after work. The biggest culprit in this is the naive person. Many take advantage of his feelings of goodness and use them at work. Even if it is a wrong feeling, the person in front takes advantage of himself. People are fooled by the nature of innocence but no one thinks that they think of everyone. The family is also responsible for much of the emotional damage. Since Lada's son is at home, all his needs are taken care of by his parents. This feeling is not wrong at all but the biggest question is what their children gave them and what they should give in return. If you pay one hundred percent, at least the person in front of you must pay sixty to seventy percent for you. And no one learns all these feelings before, but they can always come in after coming into this world. They change with age. How a person handles these mysterious feelings depends on his or her self-esteem. There are so many things happening in the world of social media right now that every single news item that is spread in the air is widely spread even without knowing how much truth there is. The person she is talking about doesn't even think about how much it can hurt her. And they have no idea that this person is a member of our own family or that we can live in this world. Even a person who spreads news about another has no idea. That person we can live in tomorrow. The basic premise is that when we hear a story four or five times, it starts to feel real, even if it is false. Because we have so much faith in it that our emotions force us to accept it. People often try to make sense just by hearing that it is not as it seems at all, but it is still not understood as it should be. Unless a person travels through that feeling, he will never know. Basically, people have never thought about the effect that anger can have on a person, how much it can affect him, how much it can hurt his feelings, how much it can hurt him and hurt his soul. This thing has no purpose. The biggest sin for that is "suicide". It is a sin because there is no such thing as suicide. When simple things take over the mind, and when those feelings are not tolerated, the person commits suicide. There is no harm in the person who is obsessed with things, but the person who loses his life is a suicidal person. But this is not the way to go. And it can never be the way. There is no harm in losing just one person. Hill will cry for four days and forget about him on the fifth day. In fact, if there is one thing that makes sense in accepting a thing properly, it is this. That human being understands every emotion a different kind of emotion. It means that there is a different kind of value hidden in each emotion. In fact, it is something that everyone has an idea of. But more importantly, every emotion is temporary. When something goes well, his happiness lasts for a few days, after which he begins to feel as usual. Sadness is the same, even if it is very sad, it lasts for a few days, then after that, according to that feeling, its intensity decreases day by day. If there is a quarrel with someone, we give a lot in anger. After a few days, the intensity of the quarrel decreases. This change is like a mysterious change. So the real meaning is that there is no need to go too deep into any emotion. And everyone should always remember that it shouldn't play with anyone's feelings because you can't even guess how deep that feeling has taken him. We can also earn virtue by doing good deeds. But the sin that comes through emotion stays with us for a lifetime. So, in this life, one should go ahead and talk to each person affectionately and if possible, keep oneself at home in such a work that one should not have much time to live in any emotion. Because the world today is such that everyone has to work hard to be successful in their own world, so they have to live every moment, but they have to move forward with the feeling that they do not have to push themselves completely.

Chapter 3 – love

Another important element in human life is "love." Every person in life has at one time or another fallen in love with someone. It also has many forms that are always alive in a changing form. Not only that, it doesn't take a certain period of time for love to happen, but it can happen to anyone. And the most important thing is that if there is one emotion that has the most power, it is love. No matter how intense the argument may be, when you try to win something with love, it becomes easier. If there is one thing that can help you in life, it is love. On a day when you can't express in words how much you love a person, you need to understand that you love him or her very much. Those who love us so much never express themselves in words. For example, your parents always work hard for you, and always work hard to give your child a better life. But even when they do not express it in words, they realize how great their love is. It is not only man who is loved. Love is also the key to animals. Not only that, man also loves animals so much that he sometimes expresses his feelings for them in words. And it is clear from their movements that animals also have emotions. There are many instances in which when a pet owner leaves this world he does not even eat for two days. If this is not love then what to say. Love is also expressed at different stages as it is said that in the year of the person we love the most we are also very angry at the person because we are worried about him and there is love somewhere in the anxiety. It is said that when each other's worries grow, love grows even bigger. Love that comes from the heart is never a lie. It is not a bad feeling at all for a person to fall in love with such a person, it is a wrong feeling that when you make a wrong decision through love that hurts others. I mean, your family has to go through a lot of things according to that, people have to listen to four things, that thing goes wrong. You make that decision because your love is understood somewhere. Not only this, with the help of love you can do great things. Not only does love make many people believe, but it is so terrible that he doesn't even try to fall in love with any person from the next time. So that there will be no time to endure that pain again. But not everyone is the same and has bad feelings. The pictures in front of him reveal what kind of people he lives with, what kind of company he goes in, his emotions, his thoughts become daily. The biggest misconception of many people is that love and attraction are mostly seen in two things. There is as much difference between love and attraction as there is between earth and sky. Attraction is limited to a few days. After a few days, as the intensity of attraction decreases, the attraction also decreases, but the feeling of love is made up of such strong threads. Not even. And for that he always tries to hold on to it. But in the present situation, the world is surrounded by selfishness. The consequences of fraud are widely accepted. So easily no one loves anyone because there are many reasons behind it like greed, money, selfishness etc. Because of greed, many families have lost their love for each other. So even if people are fooling the villagers, it is available in large quantities due to their low needs. People in the city do not understand this because their change is increasing day by day. As a result, their love is sometimes limited to their needs. So many types of love can be experienced accordingly. The biggest losers are those who love people from the bottom of their hearts. And their love is hidden somewhere in the world of selfishness. We see human love even through dry empathy, but it is difficult to tell whether it is love or something different. A person who finds it easy to tell the difference between love and affection should understand that he has a lot of experience in this regard before so he can divide it into hypocrisy and love. For example, the color of sugar and salt looks the same from a distance, but there is a big difference in their taste. The world is changing day by day and the simple world is not the same as it is now. So it is not possible to predict when someone will come and insult your love, so it is not important to love anyone except your friends and family. Because the feeling of love is also like a reflection. If you give love to the person in front of you today, then tomorrow he will try to give it to you in a big way. If you give grief, you will get grief for the rest of your life. It is essential that you know the nature of each person involved, that each person involved is a different form and made up, so it may not be possible to give him the same kind of love. In fact, human beings should start talking about love by convincing themselves of their needs and responsibilities as well as living every moment. Because out of all these mysterious changes there is a change. If you ever decide to stay with someone, you should not forget your family by mistake because they are the people who make you what you are today. Even though it is a simple and straightforward thing, many people have largely forgotten about it. On which she thinks of herself today only and only when she has a lot to do with her happiness. Even though many reasons for love are so important and with him, he has become so blind in this world that he cannot even guess what should be accepted and what should be forgotten.

Chapter 4 – Specialist

As a person tries to understand the world in detail day by day, he comes across a lot of facts related to various things and their superior emotions. His interest is decided accordingly. Many people choose their own field of interest, and try to build a career accordingly. Not only that, but many people have to worry about choosing a career that suits them. But the important thing is, do you really want to do what you do? If you are doing whatever you want, it is very difficult and it has a different kind of curiosity and a different kind of happiness. Not only this, with the help of fire you can do welding. But the worst thing is when you are forced to do something even when you are not interested in it, you do not want to do it even if it is a simple task, which also reduces your desire to go somewhere. And one of the most mysterious changes in all of this is the "expertise." It is designed in a special way. Which is not a natural thing, nor is it a matter of man-made clouds. And the implication is that if a person is adept at what he is already adept at, it is not at all that he is adept at it. And no person easily becomes proficient in any field, he gives himself time, gives time and also works hard and after hard work, he gets the fruits in the form of mastery. For example, if a young person tries to learn to ride a bicycle, he often loses his balance. But his frequent injuries make him just as strong and he learns to ride smoothly. The first reason for this success is his love. If he had not had the desire to learn to ride his bicycle through that hobby as well, he probably would not have thought of it with such mastery, and so he would have been deprived of education. The important thing is that learning to cycle is not an art. You can't make anyone attractive with his help, but learning is important, and with that much joy and desire, his desire is fulfilled through a deep wound in his mind. And the passion is the same as the master, it doesn't come already The juice they made in that area, the passion they created in their minds, the passion is the same. There is no point in creating a forced passion.

 A person who has a great deal of interest in what he loves, strives to master it, and when he becomes proficient, he enters the battlefield. And if for example he got that 3rd position. So two things are divisive, one is that he is not as happy as he should be. And secondly, he will be very happy. There is nothing wrong with either. The thing is, the joy in his heart. If he is not as happy as he wants to be after the third number, then he must be thinking somewhere that we can become more proficient. We need to become more proficient. . But even if you are happy with the heavy third number, it means that you do not need as much morale as you want, there is so much for you. It can also mean that you have limited your life plan. An important factor that comes with mastery is the dream. The implication is that a person who can dream big can certainly fulfill it. If he has the things he loves, the things he loves, he has chosen his career and he has also dreamed of a field, then all he needs to do is work hard and his dream can come true. But for that he has to face a lot of these things, that is, he will not get as much taste as he wants until someone comes against him. Because if he is in your delusion, there is no one like me, one day he will be greatly harmed by this Brahma. Because being proficient means in this way it can be said that he is the king of that field. And he is also called an artist in quality language. And so far no one was able to send in the perfect solution, which is not strange. And the same person is confronted by the person who, without ignoring his own mistakes, changes them and corrects them by making mysterious changes. And when a person grows up and his dream comes true and his inner art, that is, the art in which he excels, comes before the people in all respects, his art, hard work, failure is greatly appreciated. The fun of his art is provided until he succeeds. But when you make fun of someone in life, you should also think that if that joke happens to you tomorrow, you should bear it. The good news is, wait until the fun is over. And in life, it is possible to make fun of anything, but it should never make fun of a person's dreams, as well as his situation. It is the dream of every parent that their child should become a great person by getting good education in studies but this does not happen at all because it can never happen that every person or every person has the same ability in studies. Because the message that God has given us is wisdom, but the intellect of many people cannot tell us from what point of view they can develop their interest in anything. Some people are basically very smart but they can't master it because they are not interested in the study. But even the thing you love is going to be honest if you are not ready to do it in a month, it will be a dream come true. In the present situation, it cannot be said that study is everything, you are basically interested in it and if you are always able to choose it, then you have to work hard to bring about your mysterious change. Because mastering every field is not an easy task.

In fact, it is important to know the basics in order to be truly proficient. In fact, when a person realizes the courage to become proficient in something, he goes after it. So be careful that the mysterious changes in your future career do not become dangerous. In fact, the dream is the same when we run after it to become proficient. So it's time to dump her and move on. And this has naturally happened to most people. Rarely do people find the guidance they need in order to become proficient in life. Basically, when a guide comes to me through simple, people rarely respect him. If not, many people give up the idea of boredom. And this is the law of creation. Man's mind also takes a different turn accordingly over time. Most of the time that change goes in the right direction, but something goes wrong. So no matter how you make a decision, it doesn't matter how much you change your career. But the person who helps you the most to become proficient is the one or the other guide in your life to whom you can also give the status of a lamp. There are a lot of people who don't have a reason for it, but somewhere or other it is because of them that you have become proficient in those things.

Chapter 5- Purpose

There is a law of creation, the creature, we always think about what work we start, why we are doing that work. What is behind a certain kind of hidden element is called purpose. There are many reasons why you can make a mysterious difference at a certain stage in your life. In this case, it is often difficult to understand, if a deceitful person suddenly starts talking well to you, when a stingy person suddenly starts giving to you, the person who always does what you do suddenly starts supporting you. There are a number of reasons why change can make you look skeptical. And that dubious part is very important because when there is a sudden change in the person in front, the motive behind it may also be different. No one can change so easily. This change in him can sometimes put us in danger. Sometimes when a person speaks to us affectionately, there is a natural butt in his speech. Naturally you have been looking for a long time but when a person suddenly starts treating you well then surely he needs some help from you. That is the purpose behind it.

Having never made a phone call in ten years, the householder should always be wary of sudden phone calls. The reason behind this is that the result of any class would have rained down on that day, so he would have called without thinking about the result. One thing that can be achieved from these things is how much less you value them than listening to your results. And if you have a large number of points, the phone will not last long. This is something everyone should keep in mind. Because there is a different motive behind their calling. For this, the most scientifically come mobiles. While this person expresses his thoughts through social media, his fluent speech, his fluent language draws attention to a lot of things from here. A lot of people also think that they have won because of their rhetoric, but if a person is only hurting because of your behavior, and his soul is being hurt somewhere, then that rhetoric is never made to win. From this the person is judged. What is their original purpose behind that is addressed. It is a very wrong feeling and it is very wrong. There is no one else but you. Such a change in a human being occurs only when his maturity is lacking somewhere and because of a certain kind of pride, this mysterious change is seen in him. Wrong feelings are in the hands of many people and he tries to change it but it doesn't happen the way you want it to. So man should try to assimilate those things which will be very useful for his future. For example, if a person likes showy life very much in the world, then if he is working hard in the sound of that showy life, then surely he will work hard step by step because of that sound of fear. Not only that, but a lot of people work hard at what people will say to them, because people don't have to say anything to them. The point is, bad habits, even weaknesses, can make you stronger on the road to success. If you find a scholar, he will say that you have to give up these bad habits and you have to give them up. Most of the rubbish left in the house is discarded. The same researchers come and do research on it and they turn that waste into good architecture. It can also be said that each person's attitude towards the object and the motive behind it is different. Due to the current differences as well as the atrocities being perpetrated on them, even ordinary people fall prey to them, even if there is nothing wrong with them, it would have been time for them to go to jail. But when they come out, it's time for them to explain to themselves that their motive is often to say that we are not what you think we are. Sometimes life forces us to understand. That is to say, right now yoga is filled with a certain kind of selfishness. In such a situation, the faith of many people has also risen, and not only that, but hatred is now seen in every person. But the point of view of man is that his purpose behind it is very important. If I make mistakes in every person, I will be alone in life, even if someone breaks the relationship by telling a lie, you will always be alone, so your reaction is not always important for what I think. No one but you can understand what the purpose is. But with that being said, if I am trying to maintain your relationship, then of course you can try to live a better life not only today but also tomorrow. Because a lot of people live with the thought that if something bad happens to them today, it will be bad forever, but there is a big difference between day and life. Every day you have many goals that make you happy. They also create a lot of motives in front of you that you can only be miserable for the rest of your life. Now it's up to each individual to see how he or she tries to bring about these changes. So both your eyes should always be the same and their eyes should also be in the same vision, because your eyes today help you to understand a certain kind of purpose for tomorrow's future. It also inspires you to learn a certain kind of story from the moment you live in your mind. Not only this, with the help of this knowledge you can do great things in life. If you keep the mistakes of the past in mind, you will never be able to find a better future, so keep in mind the intention of forgetting the mistakes of the past and making the future better. If it reminds you of past mistakes, you can ignore them and deal with them. Frequent mistakes will only lower your morale, because mistakes made by people will not change your future as well as your future. You want to change those mysterious changes. And with that in mind, your goal should be to have a strong vision.

Chapter 6- Injury

In addition to the many delightful things, mysterious change is another emotion that can cause a great deal of change. At the age at which we live, we know that food is not easy. Because we don't know the purpose behind it. Because your feeling is hurt, I was thinking through that feeling. So the memories become like putting your feet on the extreme thorns. Everybody knows that if you want to live a good life and create a happy future, then you have to forget the mistakes of the past and forget the sorrows of the past, otherwise you will not be able to welcome the future well. But it is easy to say but very difficult to understand. Injuries never have the desired effect. When we think of the past after moving into the future, it has a huge impact. Therefore, as the seasons change, so does the human being. So a person who has a great deal of self-control over his own feelings is never easily hurt. But every person has a point of view, that is, but if a person looks at anything from a particular point of view, it has two aspects. In her famous language they are called negative and positive. In fact, if a person with a positive attitude looks at the injury, he learns something from it, rather than suffering. It is also very important to have one's own mindset to understand it. And if that mentality is developed today, then tomorrow it will be of great benefit to the person. And it is inevitable that tomorrow you will laugh at the things that made you sad today. And it is not a bad thing to learn something, it just matters how it leads you to success. And the other person who looks at the injury with a negative attitude is the one who stays in the same grief and pulls himself into a very unfortunate attitude. they make up their minds that nothing good can happen now but these people forget that it was a day, it was a bad time in your life, but at the same time they transform the day into a whole life, that's for sure Everything is a sad storm that will happen for some time.

Man also has a certain attitude towards injury and no one can see the attitude without him. The implication is that each person has a specific type of grief. Some people are aware of their grief in a certain way, while some people do not even know the difference between what kind of grief should be taken on their head and what kind of grief should be forgotten. It is a well-known fact that when a person is very important to you, even the smallest thing can hurt you. And even if the person you never pay attention to says something bad to you, you don't pay attention to him or her at all, because he or she is not important to you. So it is very difficult to predict which person will be important and which person will be useful to you as much as you have restraint on your emotions because when we travel in emotions, there is no journey in it, we just fly in it like a river which has some kind of way to stop. Does not exist. Mysterious changes have a profound effect on this. When a person is very important to us today, when a person comes into our life after him and when he is even more important than that person, the influence of the previous person is lessened somewhere, so we do not pay attention to the injuries caused by them. What if not this mysterious change?

Also, the story of the injury comes from the mysterious revenge, while the factor that helps to bring about another change along with the injury is "over-thinking". The most thoughtful part of this group is over-thinking. In fact, it hurts us to think of things that wouldn't have happened, even if it was done with a lot of imagination in our heads. But if things are not checked properly, then what are you upset about? For a certain reason, they think that they have hurt themselves by thinking a lot about something that has not happened. And one study found that when a person is truly traumatized, two changes take place, one being that the person becomes very rude. Otherwise if the person transforms himself into peace due to the large amount of maturity. His calmness makes many things happen as he tells the world. If your reaction to everything is a significant injury, then there is no need to express happiness in front of everyone. And not only that, if you are hurting yourself because of the injury, there is no greater pain because it will not affect the person or the things that did not hurt you.

The human experience is strong only when it experiences a greater variety of things than the good ones. And everything depends on the person's thoughts and behavior, so why should a person be in a good mood and not even create stress by not reacting to the injuries that come with it? Also, when a person's mood is always sad, his attitude towards good things is always expressed according to the hurt. And the more difficult the problem, the stronger it becomes. And yet if you try to hurt someone by saying bad things, this will never be your victory. In fact, even a small quarrel can make many people make a big mistake by pretending to be hurt. And they will repent for the rest of

their lives. Even with the knowledge that this is
a feeling at times. But the person I love doesn't
care about the person in front of them, it
doesn't mean they don't feel angry, it doesn't
mean they don't feel bad at all, they feel bad
too, but they stay with you for the rest of their
lives because they love him. . Because the love
that accompanies them weakens the other hurt
This way many mysterious changes can be made
according to the injury so you should always use
your injuries carefully if possible not to declare
yourself injured at all if not needed. The grief
that is not yours, now pulling yourself into grief
also forces you to make yourself anxious.

Chapter -7 Discretionary thinking

If you have nothing to do, then one of the most important tasks you can do is to think. But the thoughts and I are formed according to the events of your mind, most of the if you can ignore but your mind is surrounded by it, so that those thoughts are mixed in your mind at every moment. Therefore, it is said that if the mind is distracted by taking many thoughts into its head, there is only one way out of this confusion. He should keep himself busy as much as he can, so that he does not get confused in his mind. If the life There can never be a full stop in this life I have no means to stop your thoughts. There are so many people who make such a plan in their mind that they never even think about whether it will last that long or not. Therefore, it is said that the past tense and future tense should be mentioned more in the present tense, because the past is gone and the future tense is coming, yet think that the past tense and future tense are more than the present tense. But there is more to it than meets the eye. It is said that every person in this world is always at work but this will always make it come true, not at all. Because man is a person and no matter how much you employ, the machine will never be able to do so much work itself. So one should make it a habit to spend five to ten minutes a day reading a conscience.

Conscience thinking is not a period that is limited to just a few days. It can be an important part of your life as well as your career in a very important way. It can even cause a certain kind of change in our thinking. There is nothing wrong with thinking that most people have low levels of thinking. The behavior of the people around him was influencing his thinking. In fact, it is a very important factor for young people to come out and get out of their confusion. Not only that, if your identity is hers today and if your identity has a certain kind of ink on it, then yes or no, today will be a day of conscience thinking to change your thinking, future life can change.

The world has been evolving from a different perspective since 2000. I don't know, but as before, there was intimacy, people had affection for each other. Somewhere along the way it has been declining. It is not at all a pleasure to meet. But there was a heart in my heart. That moment was becoming a very important memory. One of the most important things for a person to have a good conscience is to get a good education. And the price of education is for everyone, rich or poor. So no matter how much a person goes forward, or even if he has immense wealth, he should not give up education. It is very important to take education to make a difference in the thinking Saini because education is another identity of yours. You don't need anyone's advice to put your conscience into practice. Your experience is enough to make that mysterious change happen. We try to put the thoughts of great thinkers into practice, but we do not think that the thoughts they have formed are also based on their experience. This is a great thing if you think of someone as your role model, but don't think that you can be your role model. There are also many conscientious thoughts that your mind will not like at all, some may be in addition to your mind. But the thing to keep in mind is that most of the time you don't like it, it doesn't mean it's wrong. It can be said that a person who remembers his mistakes and does not understand them according to the lesson or repeats those mistakes, has learned something new from those mistakes and moved forward today. Not every sentence is against you, or every sentence is with you at all. Even so, owning one is still beyond the reach of the average person. The pride that you get, the happiness that you get is limited to today, that is, it will remain tomorrow, it cannot be said. The person who respects you today will respect you tomorrow, the person who likes you tomorrow will not like you tomorrow.

Everything is on time. Language changes may also change over time. But the happiness that most people get and the respect that most people get if they want to survive to the end only and only express their results, here hard work is just as important but no one asks your hard work but they remember the result you gave. To give an example, "laziness is the enemy of man." This is a good idea. Most of it is also taught to that little boy after school. But as the person becomes more enthusiastic and if he becomes lazy, this idea goes wrong somewhere. But the person who has put it into practice and is more successful without it, nowhere did he put laziness along. Things are changing. Everyone knows what to do and what not to do. But if one does not try to work hard on one's own, then automatically you see change in the future.

It also means that there is no point in having 100 conscientious thoughts in the world but not putting them into practice. But if a day's thought is a matter of conscience, then by putting it into practice, we will somehow succeed in the future, and that thought will remind us of how much a thought made then has changed my future today. So this change has not happened easily, it has become a big triangle from small hard work in a row. It's just a matter of putting one's conscience into action and putting one's future somewhere in the right direction.

Chapter 8- Price

Anything bigger is appreciated by the price tag behind it. And whatever it is, it costs everything. Be it human, animal, or personality. But the price is made up of a specific form. In the case of human beings, if in the beginning it is not worth it, then you can work hard and make your own worth. But if one of his small mistakes can cost him a lot of money. Making your own price is a big deal. But there is more to it than meets the eye. Because even an example of mysterious change can be considered price. Some people set their own prices too early, and as time goes on, a lot of things happen because of the change of members, not only because their price goes down, but also because some people increase their price so much that it can't be reduced because of the anxiety they have built up. The building adorns their talents. What matters most is your self-esteem, your goals, your hard work, and your attitude towards which your self-esteem is built. It means that when people respect you a lot, you value a lot, but if someone does not respect you, they are always disrespecting you, they do not care what you think, what you share and what is your attitude towards the person. If they have no idea where they are, they want to know how much your value is. If you are not earning anything today, then your price is almost zero. But after being unemployed today, when you work for a higher salary tomorrow, your price automatically goes up. Not only that, it may take some time to appreciate when a person grows from small to big, but when someone's price goes up to a big low, people spread the word about his low price so fast. I mean, look how big the change is.

And today in every field no one is ever supported by telling. So just as every person has a point of view to look at a person, it is at their given price. For example, if there is an educated person, I would like to talk to educated people and communicate with them because they value those values. Also, these people have a large amount of people's wealth, they treat them according to the key to wealth. Now it is up to the next generation to decide what to respond to. If some people find people who share their thoughts on the things they are interested in, then giving them importance makes them interested. But it is important to remember that just as the five fingers of a hand are never the same, so too is the taste of each. Many people have different lifestyles, some people like to use these things at low prices, some people like to buy expensive things on purpose. Their symptoms change day by day. You like to have a lot of respect for the person of today, and when that person says something bad to you, you lower the value in your eyes by keeping the wrong feelings about him in mind. Socially speaking, a person who learns in a school in the district automatically falls in love with the school, and after falling in love, he also develops a fondness for the teachers there. So when we go to university for further education, the cost of school somewhere, the love for school, goes down somewhere, because now her feelings are intense, her memories are fading somewhere. Which means it's about to be the most delusional time of the year, as well. This experience must have come to 95% of people out of 100%. This instinctive change comes in a very short time. In fact, when it comes to people, the same thing applies with the , the person we talk to every day. But if after a while it goes too far and there is a gap in speech, then somewhere the price goes down. That is not to say that the value of that person has completely diminished.

Also, for example, the biggest price show is in politics. There is a very simple way. When a person is elected, he is known by four people, and around him, four people are seen respecting him. But this great and this price is limited, as long as he is elected, if his power falls tomorrow, his price will automatically decrease. And it's natural there's no disagreement.

Because in this world, that is, in this selfish view, everyone is sitting for their own benefit. Many people reduce their own cost by their own hands. The key factors are anger, naming, sarcasm, and pride. There is a great deal of pride and arrogance in today's world where one should be proud of oneself or for every good deed. There are many examples of this. For example, nowadays, it is not only insulting to call a person in front of you, but also talking to a person in front of you is a big financial loss for them. But the simple thing is, if you speak up, what's going to happen? Yet people have a different kind of craze for their own value. But the existence of such people is likely to end very soon. Because the world we live in and the current generation has a different kind of perception is that no one is hindered by anyone. So people may need a lot to bring illusions with their own minds. This is a misconception. If you ignore people, don't do it in such a way that people will respect you as much. Because selfishness is also hidden in every person, intimacy is hidden in the same way, but in life, it gives the same, if you have ever tried to play it yourself. To put it simply, the price is that when you are not there, people will take your name and praise Tulsi. And if you make a mistake while you're at it, you're going to be told. This is the real price of a person, you are remembered even when you are not there, but the good thing is, what is bigger than this? When you achieve something with your hard work, and when your success is greatly appreciated without you, it is your true value. And if the name of the person after whom people are always naming, slandering them, then you know how much they are worth. The mysterious change is in your hands, how you can create and sustain your value.

Chapter 9 - Ego

In every field, when the empire is being ruined due to some things, that is, the virus is the ego. You may have seen many people who have created their own existence from scratch. But when some people have achieved success and existence on the strength of their own destiny and also on the strength of their own deeds, they soon develop a feeling of ego. Many thinkers have also expressed their views on this. And at some point his ego only works to bring him down. Therefore, many factors like hatred, envy, ego force us to make mysterious changes in our man. The simple example is that what I can do is my pride and what I can do is my ego. And this is also a natural kind of feeling. No one gets ego easily. There is probably no one more powerful than me when it comes to what people think or when they feel inside. That's when this mysterious change happens.

The image of ego is never easily created. It is created by the enemies of our individual mentality, and the biggest fact in the world is that the enemies never change, the individual creates himself. Ego is also an enemy that a person creates by himself. The mysterious change in him leaves him on the path of repentance. And identifying one's ego is a very simple task. There is no need to identify because the person with whom we have spent a lot of time, when the feeling of ego is created in him, that feeling is reflected in his speech. There are many reasons why a person does not have the same ego at all. Some people don't feel like they have completed their definition of ego without describing everything. So no matter what the topic is, it is always important for them to have an exhibition to describe their ego. Every person in this world has a certain kind of pride in his child and he should be proud too, because for every person his son is the king. But his son can do what he should be proud of, his children should do that great work, and he should always be a great person in life. But when there is a feeling of ego, that change is hidden in the person in a certain form. Their son can, so the other's son is bad. If their son gets everything, then the other's child will get nothing. This feeling is wrong. This is a pattern of ego. When a person tries to understand the language we want to see, we should always remember that if they achieve what we are calling them today, then they should always prepare themselves mentally to bear the change that will take place tomorrow. And it is bound to happen if today you are insulting someone for their living or for their survival by your arrogant speech then he will try his best to achieve that and he will succeed. And he tells the story of the change that is taking place today. Not only that, in some places man's ego teaches him many things. And every moment in life teaches us a lot, so everyone should enjoy the moment at least once. That, of course, can change, as some journeys do this for a few moments, some are sweet, and some are rough. But everything tastes good. Because according to the habit, you create your love. Another thing applies to all areas.

 If there is one thing that is most important to us, it is our whole history, and everyone in history has made their own choices. Many people also say that not everything in history has been shown in this way. But it is good if the things of the world remain as long as the world lasts. Throughout history, people have built their own reputation. It doesn't matter if you have a reputation for it or not. We have to assimilate the things that are most pleasing to us. That is, the people who made history happen in large numbers who wrote their names in golden letters. One should always keep in mind one virtue from those people and make that mysterious change by oneself. If the story starts with ego for example, but one of the people who went through history was named Adolf Hitler. Who had largely formed one of our powers. It can also be said that they conquered the world on the strength of that power. But his end was due to his ego. People think that people commit suicide only when there is stress. But even your ego can one day force you to commit suicide. The person who was martyred never forgets. But no matter how well you do it but you have an ego, you will still feel a mysterious change while respecting you.

Concentration, and solitude, is the most peaceful environment in the present situation. It is said that in solitude the mind becomes purer and calmer. No matter what kind of thoughts come to mind, if we don't pay attention to them, we can create a very happy atmosphere. In fact, it is very important to teach your mind that you can conquer the world by living in solitude. You can succeed by living in solitude, but congratulations, you have learned to live your life. But in order to do all this, first of all, it is very important for you to have experience in every field. Because you can make decisions right now unless you have experience in every field. If from the beginning you have been working hard in solitude, then it is very natural for you to do that. But when you are under stress and decide to be alone, that decision can be a bit wrong. Because more stress can force you to create stress. Indeed, after being defeated by ego, people try to live in solitude. But the decision is very wrong because our mind is distracted somewhere. Simply put, it eats away at our very minds. So you should never be forced to create your ego. And no one should ever mistakenly think that one's faith will be broken and one's soul will be hurt by one's ego because there is no greater sin than this. Because you are the artist of your life. Every person in this world gets a chance every day when he can go from wrong to right. So it is up to the individual to seize the opportunity. Because change is about to happen. It is extremely difficult to put a permanent stop to those changes. Therefore, it is necessary to keep our ego under control at all times.

Chapter 10 - **Verses**

Hobby is also a means of human happiness. At times, he even goes to great lengths in his career. Just because you have a hobby does not mean that you get a big position. In fact, he pursues his hobbies because of his hard work and his passion. Trying to give a different look with his own hands. Because of his hard work, he enjoys the fruits of his labor in the form of success. Basically he tries to cultivate hobbies to create happiness. Quite often a mysterious change also happens, after a while the couple wants to move to another area of interest. And there he tries to pursue his hobby. One conclusion from this is that the concentration of such people cannot be said to have been formed from a completely systematic point of view. Basically, a person who perseveres and perseveres in the same thing over and over again, is considered an artist in that field. And this is our own life. Whatever you want to do, you have to do in one birth. For that, you have to make a name for yourself with a holistic approach.

Not only this, with the help of hobbies many people have found themselves in the world of dreams. Whose journey may have been limited to a dream. But the journey that some people have seen in your dreams has also taken place in their own real life. A lot of people who succeed have failed, just because of hard work and perseverance they would not have succeeded. This is another reason behind it. That they are basically interested in that thing. Until he reaches the pinnacle of his success, his hobby cannot be said to have been fully cultivated. His hobbies made his dream come true. And on the strength of hard work, it was brought before the world. No one person achieves much success in a day, just as a person's desire to pursue a hobby does not become intense. One thing I have learned from the study is that a person who wants to achieve something and does not get it easily, tries to achieve it even more intensely. Many also committed suicide through hobbies. But it is not a clean slate. They have to make such a decision because of their circumstances. What such people have in common is that their future generations will know better. When their children are provided with everything, they do not realize how much their father endured. Because their time has brought a mysterious change. In fact, man should never give up hope. Because no one has seen what will happen tomorrow. Positive Attitudes and Thoughts It can happen if you dream that the hobby you were pursuing will probably bear fruit tomorrow. Nature has also presented different elements of many such things. Influential and self-identifying, their researchers spend years researching their hobbies, understanding their hobbies, responding to different things, responding year after year, and after the results are achieved, their research is accomplished in a single day. Full.

The same kind of side effects of hobbies have also occurred in the present generation. The implication is that life tells us how to make a name for oneself through hard work. But this different meaning has been misunderstood by many people in different forms through hobbies. The first important question is what kind of hobby the person is pursuing. If he can get some useful things through hobbies, then that hobby basically became work for him. But if his time is running out and he is getting older but he is not getting the time he wants, even if the sweet sight is falling somewhere useless in his mind, then in time he should understand his own mind and give up that hobby. If he doesn't try to make a difference today, tomorrow will not be without remorse in his life. Hobbies should also not be divided by emotions. Because if we make the same transformation in emotion, it will become very difficult for a person to make this decision.

Every ordinary person in the world also has a
different time to change themselves every day.
But his decisions are also wrong somewhere
because he thinks of them emotionally. But one
thing to keep in mind is that if something goes
wrong, it will go wrong, so why not treat the
person who is right? And the thing that is right
will stay right, so why don't you do the wrong
thing. Some people also have a certain kind of
conservation that they are somewhat adept at
the area they want to go to. It only takes a little
bit of hard work then success is born for them
with a very simple approach. It all boils down to
the intensity created by each person's hobbies.
Some people even become extremely blind
through unwanted hobbies, this also seems to
be somewhat wrong. If you are sacrificing
everything to meet your needs, then if this
sacrifice is causing trouble to other people, then
surely your hobby is having a wrong passion
somewhere. Everyone knows this until today
when we do not announce the results for what.
Not only this, with the help of fire you can do
welding. Until then, your hobby is limited to

your Pacific. If you are also satisfied with that, and if you are pursuing your career in different fields with passion, then surely your life is living happily somewhere. So it is not important that you pursue your hobby by looking at any person. Your passion should be more natural than artificial. You should try to cultivate this area with love in your heart. Making fun of yourself by looking at others is foolishness. Because there is no definition of hobby choice. It's just like love, you never know when you will fall in love. Some people have a hobby that they don't even want to see in the future.

So this life is our own, it will be better to make our own decisions, we will not get success because of what others say. Not only this, with the help of hobbies mentioned by others, it is not always possible for us to become interested in it and fulfill our desire to cultivate it. Therefore, even through hobbies, invaluable changes take place in life. Which can be called mysterious change. Anything that is achieved by force is never achieved, so parents should pay close attention to this. He should not force his children to pursue hobbies in areas where he does not want to be interviewed. With that you can experience and even imagine the specific direction in which the mysterious change will take place.

Chapter -11 REFLECTION

What "reflection" means, most people know after hearing this word is that when we stand on the edge of the lake and look at the lake and when they see our own picture, what happens is called reflection. In fact, this is exactly the definition. Which has been done in an extended form. The structure of this thing is also understood by every person exactly. But there are many factors that make people unaware that change is not a form of perspective and that even mysterious change is a major motivator for enlightenment. The way people think differently is changing day by day because of the large number of factors around them. Today, instead of making decisions on his own, he is suddenly trying to water down the things that are happening around him. In fact, the competition is so fierce that one has to look at one's surroundings, but one's perspective is also changing. Simply put, we can say that this is a bit silly. It still lacks much of what to think about. Even in the face of so much competition and inflation, any parent wants their child to go to the level they want and make a name for themselves. Not only this, with the help of fire you can do welding. But from the point of view of ability, he can go in the field where every individual and every student wants his style, but it depends on his ability to make a name for himself. Not all parents have such complaints, but some parents see the reflection of any adult in their child, and try their best to make it accordingly. If the person recruiting students has that ability from that point of view, then surely he will come first in it and surprise everyone and on that day you can say that it is a matter of reflecting and waiting for that person somewhere. But things get worse when a person has to choose the area under the pressure of his parents and surroundings without taking the area as per his mind. While there are times when you have to go back in the field even under the circumstances, there are some students who have to leave the field of interest according to the circumstances. The implication is that the person we see reflected in the students may be even more influential. And he may want his own reflection in another person. But who has time to watch this? Everyone wants to walk according to the people around them and move forward according to what the people around them have done. The mistake that can easily get your claim denied is to fail. The mistake that can easily get your claim denied is to fail. Therefore, it is not appropriate to give the area that the student wants by force. It is not wrong to look at one's own reflection, but the lack of one's own ability is sudden or it may lead to failure. As a child, when a student looks right, it helps him to adapt to the people around him, just like when a potter shapes pots according to his own hands. So when a child is a student, he is treated according to the people around him. He often behaves and often has bad consequences. Which means it's about to be the most delusional time of the year, as well. Now it will be important for the student to know which person he is referring to.

There are many different types of component of each thing. Not only that, in some ways they are positive and in some ways they are negative. The reflection is similarly created by our various elements. Just as some reflections have also come to the fore through nature. For example, when a poor student and a child suffers a lot of atrocities and remembers those atrocities, when his name is registered among the most successful people, he tries to use his own force on the people who get rid of the atrocities committed against him. And a famous scientist had said that (Every action I have there is an equal and opposite reaction.) There is also the implication of telling, which is also often called coincidence. But it is not a coincidence that our karma sometimes treats us accordingly. For example, if you respect the other person, he will also try to present it, but if you always do it yourself, it will not take long for a hatred to form in your mind. And that's how big the reflection is. The one who introduces us to our virtues will one day give us results. But it is said that one should always be humble with everyone. But over time, that is likely to change. The feeling of belongingness is diminishing day by day. Because in earlier times human needs were less. But man's needs are now so great that he has to change color over time. One has to create a mental image of each person through different perspectives. And that's why everyone in the world wants to change the world but not change themselves. One such element of reflection is "family." Parents who see the reflection in their children today that a child raised from childhood will fulfill the dream of his parents and not only fulfill their needs but also serve them for the rest of their lives, will have the same dream today and the same reflection will be found in their child. But not only that, their faith is being undermined to a great extent by the fact that nowadays love is seldom seen as it should be. Somewhere the rites do not happen as they should. So this reflection is also sometimes misinterpreted. Many times man also gets to learn a lot through amazing reflection. What really matters is how closely we observe things. The way we look at each person is different and it is rare. But a person who chooses the right thing by dividing it into right and wrong, will have some reflection. If you think he is right to make a mistake, then he is absorbing the wrong consequences that have befallen him somewhere. Which in the future will give him nothing but loss.

Even so, owning one is still beyond the reach of the average person. So the simple and easy answer is no. Because this is a new stopping miracle. You can try to make a lot of changes in it, but you can't completely eliminate it.

Chapter -12 BEHAVIOUR

Another important factor in the so-called mysterious changes in the changing course of human life is the behavior of human beings. Even simple human behavior is changing day by day. That change is also due to the people around him. Most of the time he tries to treat her the way he treats her. In fact, it is very important for you to make changes in your behavior if you think from one point of view. Because the people around you don't treat you the way you treat them. The respect you receive and often the insults you receive will also be a factor in your behavior. But basically people most of the time like the behavior of those people, who always appreciate them. But even if someone is praising for no reason, most of them are noticed. Not only that, but in that case also it is understood what kind of treatment is being given to the person in front. According to some studies, it is also understood that if you are a child, if he is treated badly by his parents as a child, then wrong rites are done about it. And the same rites remained forever. Man can change his behavior, but it is impossible to change his original nature.

Behavior is also made up of certain types of facts. Some people run it according to their own whims, while some people act according to their natural instincts. The only difference is that some people behave artificially in front of the world. When they don't even want to behave like that, then it is natural for some people to behave according to their heart. From this it is clear that if you are natural, you do not need to work hard in your behavior, but if you are trying to make your behavior look good in order to show it to others, then you have to work hard, you have to change it. Then it starts to feel natural. You too can be deceived. That is why it is said that people should behave as they really should. But it is not possible. In the year 2022, man has to face many things, so it is not always possible for him to stay natural. Because of the way he treats, he has to make changes according to his liking. So often its artificial change is transformed into a natural change. Its artificial behavior is transformed into natural behavior. People also judge your image by your behavior. If, for example, you treat everyone with humility, the person in front of you will not even dare to criticize you. I mean, look at how important your behavior is to your image, and the people of the world right now hold their image for the same people. Even your smile reveals a lot of interpretation of your behavior. Sometimes people will forget you after praising you, but if you have been insulted, the person in front of you will never forget the behavior. It can't even make the mysterious change you want in it. So one thing to keep in mind is that there is only one life. And in this one life, every person should speak kindly and ask for humility. So that no one's soul will be hurt. If the person in front of you decides to be happy with your behavior, what could be bigger than this?

The whole important structure is expressed only through behavior, not at all. Because in many places, change is needed. As an example, it is natural to say that no matter how much a person treats you, you should not treat him with humility. So that in the future he will be ashamed of it. This is naturally true. But in reality it cannot be completely agreed upon. Because man also has feelings, he also feels bad somewhere, he also stumbles somewhere in the corner of his heart. There is a need to change your behavior somewhere, not completely. So there is an easy and straightforward way to do this, that is, to treat the people in front of them as they are. However, studies have shown that when a person is treated accordingly, he or she is more likely to be irritable. Because such a nature does not tolerate him. If the person in front of you is always rude, then how can he be tolerant if we treat him in the same way? So most human beings should behave sensibly. And to make sense of it, he has to travel through the realm of practical knowledge,

MYSTERIOUS CHANGES IN LIFE

higher education, and every event, which will
surely help him to get acquainted with the real
world. The most important factor in behavior is
one's self-esteem. Because a person's self-
esteem can be determined by the way he treats
them. Just like a person who always insults you
and always treats you at a lower level, even if
you have a different kind of affection and love
for this person in your mind, this is a big deal.
But it turned out to be a very wrong thing to do.
Because instinctively, it is impossible for you
and that person to ever be treated with respect.
But there are many things that have to be
endured in order to maintain a relationship.
This will show that you are taking care of your
mentality somewhere. Not only this, with the
help of fire you can do welding. It is often said
that this is the true meaning of burning up of
bad psychic imprints. The person in front of
them is always treating them badly, ignoring
them and keeping them in good behavior. And
after a while, she felt ashamed of him, and that
change took place in him. Even people today
treat them well. Such mysterious changes often

have to be put into practice. Some changes are very difficult but important but just as much.

Man's rage is also sometimes expressed with intense intensity through the rays, if the society is a very good friend of two persons, but in rage sir they had a quarrel. There are also frequent insults. But what no one knows about this is that it is not a misbehavior, but a specific aspect of the situation, expressed through your emotions. Because the person we always love is sometimes treated with anger, but that doesn't mean the person is insulting, or treating the person in front of us the wrong way. If you keep thinking like this, few people in your life will be behind you. Therefore, in matters of behavior, it must always be brought to a place where mysterious change must take place. If you treat anyone like that, you will definitely fall somewhere, so the people who are important in your life should be treated with that important attitude, because it is not discrimination of any kind. So the symptoms are also determined by the behavior. And people who are very respectful of your behavior should be especially careful not to offend anyone.

Chapter 13 - Disciplined

Just as mysterious changes in human life continue to happen day by day. Accordingly, there are many changes in the behavior of human beings. There is more to it than meets the eye. Many people have experienced many forms of discipline. It is also divided into two important and common perspectives. Such as artificial and natural for example. Some people basically learn discipline and assimilate it. Then some people naturally try to act accordingly. Wrong feelings but not both. In fact, every parent who sends their child to school wants their child to be disciplined. And it is the duty of every teacher and their parents to nurture children. But for most people, forcing them to be disciplined is a time-consuming and boring affair. As long as the student does not try to change himself, that is, he does not try to discipline himself, it cannot be said to have been of any use. Therefore, it is the job of the teacher and his parents to make the turn, but it depends on the student to try to bring that discipline in the student by assimilating it. Basically, man can be happier living as a human being. But with a lot of discipline, rules and etiquette, he has become a robot in modern times. He is called a robot because he is not willing to do whatever you do. And people are just making rumors, man is just an irritated animal.

Much has been expressed through this research. One of the important findings of this study is that it takes 21 days to learn something new, basically nothing happens all of a sudden. For that you have to take a step forward somewhere. Once you have a little bit out of your comfortable life, you can go and make discipline a friend. Sometimes it seems that the artificial endeavor is often transformed into a natural one. There is a reason for doing something, so making love is basically expressing one's desire. So if you want to learn discipline, you must try to do it with the utmost

care. Also, the benefits of being disciplined are
that you don't have to worry about any new,
difficult tasks. Not only this, with the help of
fire you can do welding. Now, according to the
state of mind of a person, that discipline comes
in time. Doing the same thing every day, at the
same time, in the same way with people, makes
you feel bored. But those who engage
themselves in that work. They don't find any
work boring. There are a lot of disciplined
people who have a habit of ticking the clock,
working hard, not only that, they have a set
time, they have a different plan of what should
happen at what time, that is, their daily routine.
Everyone understands that everything was fine
with such people. But do you know what
happens to the mystery that happens to them?
They work on time, they work according to the
clock, but the people with whom they have
daily relationships who push their work
forward, if not punctual, the disciplined people
suffer greatly.

Through discipline, people are really respected. The implication is that they are respected in a big way. When their lives are told in their language about their reactions and their good habits, their discipline is also described. In fact, it attracts people even when it is disciplined by many people, that is, it attracts them to motivate them in big places. Many people do not even know what kind of life they still have. Most people have a misconception that being disciplined means being well-dressed, well-groomed, and well-mannered. But basically the definition of disciplined does not allow this to be complete. If a person has made a routine of his own, if he is doing 95 per cent of the daily wholesale according to his daily routine, then that person can be said to be disciplined. But if a person starts his day without a routine and does not even know what to do now, every minute he has to think, it means he is stuck somewhere in his life. And not only that, for the rest of his life, he will have to be prepared to face things. And people talk about how much struggle there is in that person's life. But it does not consider who caused the storm of conflict. It is a fact that maturity is not always attained by age but is always based on one's experience. So there is no conflict in any person's life. Mysterious change is coming sometime. But when four out of a hundred people succeed, you look at their history once, they would have made mistakes too, the struggles would have come a long way in their lives too, but ignoring those things, according to the routine they made themselves, Change is the mysterious change that will lead them to success in the future. There is an age of hard work, but if a person works hard at any age, he will not get the same strength as usual. It's the same with discipline. If you become disciplined as time goes on, it may not be 100% useful. And time is more important than money. Money will come and go in your life for a while but once the time passes it will not come again. If you are disciplined for that, then time planning can also be done well. During the exam when the student stays up all night, and after a while when the result comes. The sleep mode during the exam gives him a good night's sleep after the result tomorrow. When a person comes home, he sleeps soundly day and night, sparingly during the month. In the wrong way, if you open your eyes 24 hours a day and get money, twenty four minutes, but sleep is always scary. So discipline is in the hands of anyone, because the grape may change. Now it's up to the individual to decide what kind of change he wants. If you want to reach your peak, you have to be disciplined.

Chapter -14 -Conclusions of changing things

What does it mean to have a changing life in every person's life? This is the most important question. But he has to change his mind accordingly. Not only this, with the help of these things you can do wonders for your life. And there are things that happen to him naturally. There are many examples of saying, for example, if one person eats only one vegetable every day, then there are things that happen with it. On the one hand, he will get bored, and on the other hand, he will find himself confused and find life very boring. So the most important thing is that man needs a new taste every time, and when he gets a new one, he will have a different kind of fun. It is not at all the case that a person changes at his own will. According to his destiny, he brings about change in himself due to many things like people he gets in life, their company. Not only this, with the help of fire you can do welding.

A well-known anthropologist has shown that
the reason why most people who are extremely
intelligent get hurt so quickly, is because the
intelligent person uses things related to
anything in a structured way. And not only this,
with the help of fire you can do welding.
Which, of course, made the video an overnight
sensation. So it is said that if you want to be
happy, you must not think too much about
things. In fact, your brain needs to be so strong
that it doesn't make any difference to you. But
most of the time the brain does not think at all.
Your tomorrow will also force you to think
about most things at this time. Basically most
of the time everyone has the same situation,
not always the same situation but most of the
time the situation is the same. So the change
that takes place in such a case is a mysterious
change, but the reaction of man, which brings
that change to the people in a more specific
form. No matter who gets first place in any
exam, he is not as happy as the person who got
third place. What would you say to the miracle

that happened? One thing is for sure, how much you have is more important than how much you have and how happy you are. Because perhaps there is nothing more pleasing than the happiness of the mind.

A person who has never made mistakes in life will never be able to understand things properly. In fact, it can even be said that a person will never make progress. And the person who will never try for fear of being happy. So his life is going to change a lot. For this, he has to prepare himself immensely. And if you think about it, it is difficult unless it is difficult for you. The more you try, the harder it will be to make things easier, and the mistakes you make in the past will not change your future. Therefore, keeping in mind the shortcomings of past mistakes, you will never be able to meet such a bright future according to the rays of the coming sun. The only thing I regret when I hear people talking about the success of such a future is that "if I had tried a little then and worked hard and stubbornly, maybe life would be a little different today". Guidance yoga is practiced by many people who are experts in the field. But it is not possible to say that change in your life is what you say it is, because that past effort is your own. And it is also important to think carefully about the attitude and mindset of the person who is guiding you. You and I can't figure out what's on everyone's mind But one can certainly make a guess. For that we have to take the knowledge of that thing completely. There are some similar findings and deals with mentality. For example, after a quarrel with a person, one of the thoughts that comes to the mind of the space people is, this is no longer my friend and now I will never be able to say that, so our relationship is broken here. And in the next few years, the thought of the past and the next few years enters our head in a big way. But after a while, when the anger subsided, they both wanted to talk to each other. And in the ocean of emotions, the friendship with each other goes away over time. The mysterious change you had experienced, and the picture you had brought before your eyes, was completely destroyed. And in fact, this is the life that makes your head work so hard to see so many things. And when all goes well, everything seems simple and straightforward.

The most important thing for any positive change is that it is very important for a person to understand himself for those things. The person who admits his own mistakes is the one who comes forward in life. Successful people are in control of almost every single moment of their lives. There are people who name him that I have never done in my life. But all of these things are very strange. Like any kind of person who wants something until he gets it, he finds it unique. But after getting this, he finds it very easy. What exactly is change? As long as you don't react to the person you want, you are the most valuable thing to him. But when you do what he says, he expresses his own thoughts about everything. That person starts to think a

little less about you. Many people may have
experienced these things, but most of the time
this change is not due to words but to behavior.
And of course there's nothing wrong with that.
It is not the fault of the person in front of us at
all, it is our own fault that we expect a little
more from them. And the most important thing
is that you are a bad memory in the life of any
person who leaves this world. Because there is
no cure for these changes, these changes will
continue to happen. Which you will not be able
to reduce in any direction. How it will be
reduced will be the answer to all your questions
in the future. So the person who got it, got the
situation, we should fully participate in it and
try to solve the problems that arise.

Chapter -15 -Aspects of things

Just as there are two parts to the back of every coin, there are also many elements of life that have basically two parts behind them. But most of the time, there is a time when man does not get distracted to pay attention to the other part. Which also brings about many changes in his life. For whom they have often sat at their own expense. Because the most important thing at such a time is concentration, the attitude of understanding anything, the similarities and the seldom there are people who do not get it, I have shaped myself accordingly. At first glance, your life is very much like a bicycle, just like a bicycle, if you walk straight, it feels very different, but when your balance on the bicycle does not fit in the right time, it feels a little difficult to ride. And the change that happens is due to our behavior. In fact, at that time there was a big difference between self-understanding and the attitude of understanding. But one thing that every person has experienced is that whenever there is a time when a person has to face a big crisis, he often forgets his patience. If he thinks at such a time, if he understands the situation in crisis, if he thinks about the other side of the situation, then surely the mysterious change that takes place in his life will do his best to show the best way in the direction he wants. To be sad is to never be defeated. Defeat happens when a person does not try to get out of it. One step at a time can be a turning point in your life. But your emptiness will be like embracing defeat. There is no such thing as a bad situation in one's life. But when we see a good situation, we forget that the person has given himself a better life by running away from the situation without taking any step.

The thought of any individual or any great thinker sends a message to the world. Because you have reached that peak by experiencing the thought for yourself, learning from it and working hard on it, making mysterious changes in it. But the world only sees one side of your life coin, because they never see its back side, only you know. People don't just understand the feelings in your mind, they make many arguments on the feelings outside of you and accept them according to their mind. And that's exactly the aspect of things. Many people have a strange habit. Some unwillingly show that they do not understand at all. But when you open up to the part of them (which you don't see) you will know that they know everything, they understand everything, but when you look at their innocence or when you look at them from a non-understanding point of view, Makes a lot of things easier to achieve. In fact, one thing to understand is that most of the time people get the same intelligence, the difference is only felt when that person finds us using their intelligence. There are two things that can happen in this situation. If he uses it well, he will definitely go ahead in life and if he misuses it, he will definitely suffer in life. So it is said that you cannot base your judgment on a person's face, his condition, or his intelligence.

It can change so dramatically that no one has ever thought of it. There are many instances where a person who has lost his life in a hut builds the biggest building by failing three times in a row and finishing first for the fourth time. So these mysterious changes don't have to be argued from any aspect of things. Because every person's time is inevitable and, not only that, but the intensity of life is not the same in every person's life, just as the intensity is higher than the sun in the morning, like the moon in the evening, the brightness is in both elements, So it's just a matter of time. And every person in this world has the same life as the sun and the moon. Some will shine today, some will shine tomorrow, but only if the person who has tried to take a step forward, will shine in life.

So the thing is now in the year 2022 where people don't have that faith in individuals, through social media and news, they have a very specific belief in every word they say about what is happening. Because no one has time to look at anything from two sides, because there is no specific type of proposal that has been made on a large scale. A psychiatrist has also expressed his opinion that whenever something comes to your mind again and again, whether it is wrong or right, but your mind starts to feel it most of the time. In fact, when there is a large amount of subject matter around you, and you don't even know the exact aspect of it, the repetitive single-word bombardment makes the story stick to you. Then the conclusion of that thing is right or wrong. Because the biggest dominant factor in the current generation is the media, not only that, but it also works under the hands of the people who fill the media. It is a psalm made up of all the powers that be, how things can be presented and how things can be destroyed. Not only that, but most of the media have worked hard to give a 100 percent story, even with the help of certain elements, to shape the aspects of these things in a certain way. After two days, the world forgets the people who raised their voices against the vote. Because it doesn't matter to them. There is a natural mystical change, which is spread through things most of the time, but as an ideal citizen, one should always examine the background of the thing before believing it easily. And if you have the time to express your thoughts, you should definitely check it yourself. Because it is a huge change in the way things are heard and thought with one's head. Because most of the time, even the biggest change in a relationship is caused by a thing called misunderstanding. For that too, the thing should be checked at least once. Because when we accuse someone, we must be 100% sure, that is, try to look at the back of the coin.

Chapter -16 touch

What does "touch" mean to most people? But
most people do not realize what kind of feelings
these reactions create. Which is expressed by
emotion in every moment. Its definition will
work even if it is not known. But from what
point of view it is necessary to know. And there
are also many touches that have caused a
variety of changes. Which can make a
difference. There are some touches that give
pain to the mind and also create a new identity.
Also, some of the touches often cause damage
to the person.

 In simple terms, if we define touch, we mean
the reaction of the hand that the person in front
of us can understand by the brother. Can draw
certain types of conclusions. And with that we
can act next time. For example, if a child makes
a mistake as a child, and then just slaps him
twice on the back, he will probably never make

that mistake again. And he will always remember the touch caused by the stroke. Also, if a student passes with good marks and then his parents try to boost his confidence with a touch on the back, he will remember that touch for the rest of his life and realize that we too can be successful.

And for example, there are many things that we can perceive by touch and even perceive according to our own mind. But just as important as touching one's own mind is just as important as realizing the other. And what kind of year does it matter or not? But the touch of one thing should always be that the touch of their parents at least their hard work to teach you how to work hard for you to make you. Because not everyone is aware of this. Unless he is touched from within. And this touch is not going to get hit by any person. We should always try to find out for ourselves what our parents are up to in order to get that touch of the heart. And if their hard work does not touch your heart, what is the use of your life? If you do not understand the sorrow, happiness, their needs, their hard work, their feelings in your heart, then what kind of soil has become your heart that does not touch these things.

There are many students in the academic world who declare themselves smart through crime. And also in any academic field, you are known only by merit. If you drop out of university, your memories will be enhanced by these qualities. Be it in your exams or in your personal behavior. And the student should have a good and proud identity of his own in the whole field and not in this exam. That is, he will receive a full degree of student status. But the same person who has gone through that area knows about it. It is often the case in the academic age that the student fails. It is safe to say that this is not the case. But when he is guided by his teacher, his guru, and when he touches his mind, he passes by studying hard. And it is often the case that jokes, jokes, and many other reasons from a friend cause him to lose interest in his studies without passing them. As a result of such verbal touch, he harms himself. And why education is so important when you are in the community, because of your education you have a different identity. Your parents have a different kind of pride in you. And at the same time, you are treated differently. That is to say, having passed and being ahead in education, the benefit of taking that touch at that time was in the future.

 The "tongue" is a part of the body that Has a tongue but a very large hand. Which identifies the taste of food when touched. G is spicy, sweet, sour, or salty. Makes you aware of all these types of things. And the tongue also does the work of a sword that sometimes makes the person in front feel bad or happy. In fact, all of our organs have bones, but the tongue is used in many ways, even when there are no bones. Just like when a person is doing a good job, he tries to increase his self-confidence by praising him and also when he uses those words of praise, the touch of the words made by GB touches his mind and he tries to do even better by increasing his self-confidence. Also, if there is another person who is trying to do a good job and at the same time a person who is giving him a bad comment on the strength of bad intellect and lowers his self-confidence. But through his touch, his mind is transformed into sorrow and the decision to do good remains a decision. It shows what kind of touch it should be.

When a person builds his own world, there are many things behind it, there are also many stories. But no one thinks that when his short story comes before the world and the effort he has put into finding that character of that story, he must have enjoyed so many touches to make that minute easy. Because an artist never happens without drinking out of sorrow. And every time he has to move forward by pretending that touch, most of the time that touch can be through pain and often it can be achieved through hard work. But he can never bring the original life of that touch before the world. Because touch is a kind of made-up angle that can only be expressed through emotion, not words.

No one in this world can make you happy. Unless you are trying to be happy yourself. No one can make you successful in this world unless you strive to make yourself successful. Because in every field you get the touch you want according to your mind. The only difference is how you pull it off. And there are many things in nature that we can never change. That is impossible unless you try.

One thing is clear from all these relationships. That is, the touch is not the only way. Touch is done by most things. It is also expressed by most things but not by words but by various elements. Many touches are also related to human emotion, for example, if someone is sad, if you give him a big hug, then your words are not needed. It will not allow anomalies to develop, so look at the small action that caused this touch to reduce the rapidly growing disease of grief somewhere. And not only touch but touch is another part of our hands and feet as well. It is an example of how our eyes are very funny. This is what is expressed by touch. This means that if a child is too stubborn to ask for a toy, then his mother will show him his eyes and reduce his stubbornness and this will show that touch is also done by her. This is because as the eyes get bigger, the child is told a lot of these things. And this is what if you are aware of any touch, that is, think that it is not just a science expressed by the emotions, but the chain of the bicycle is tied to it somewhere or other related to every emotion. Much of the work is lightened by touch, in which a person does not need to speak at all. Even the touch of a human tongue can sometimes be life threatening. Which causes a lot of misunderstandings and also shocks the human heart. One of the

unforgettable things about a man is that he
never utters his own words when he is angry,
because when he comes to the area, he often
says things that take away the person in front of
him, and if he is not irritated, he is soft-hearted.
The effect that it has is touching, however,
which is very sad and stressful, which is very
wrong. When angry, man forgets his humanity
and starts behaving like a monster who, even
though he seems to have diversified and
conquered in it, always loses to the person in
front when no name or any of your situation
makes any sense. If he is speaking badly,
because the words in which your dirty words
are blowing hurt the heart of the person in front
and if that touch is created, then those words
and that situation are of no use.

The unstoppable miracle is the touch that is.
Its intensity is also high in one way or another.
Like touch, it is easy for the person around to
touch each other, but when the person moves
away, the touch is different. Some people are

also heavily touched by running. And for some
as a baby gets older, he or she will outgrow this.
It is unknown at this time what he will do after
leaving the post. This miracle will not stop now.
Everyone knows that there is no need for a
person to have the same feelings about a
person. What kind of context do they get
behind them, and what kind of touches do they
get? It is equally difficult to say exactly what is
the reason behind their nature. You cannot
experience sorrow unless it happens to you.
The touch of a few things is something you
don't realize when you help yourself. And there
are some touches that we contribute to
ourselves. There is no specific reason for
helping, but we still have to touch it to reach
our own minds by deliberately remembering it.
Some people are so obsessed with anything.
When the subject matter of that thing is not
even the beginning. They have to endure these
touches even with the extreme thinking of
human beings. Some people have no shortage
of artists, but when you hear something, the
person in front of you feels bad, and that's

exactly what the person in front of you has said. The person tries to ignore the matter without ever replying to him, but if the person does not respond in any way, it does not mean at all that he is not touched by the thing. He touches it too. The effect of that touch on his mind is that even he just doesn't want to react. And there is a huge shortage of such people in this world because nowadays people often bring their minds to the world in the matter of how to quarrel for a small reason because by listening they try to make themselves feel weak. Man cannot exist without human needs. Every person has his own needs in one form or another. And not only that, they also change from time to time. It depends on each person's thoughts, the level of his thoughts, the level at which he behaves and his needs are automatically born. As a result of the upheaval in his mind and head, man has not hesitated to understand himself on a different level. In fact, man cannot express how much he loves anyone. And the funny thing is, when you can't express your love for someone, you know how much you love them. But the simple feeling in this case is that if the pain of seeing the person's grief touches your heart, then of course you have curiosity and affection for him. And all of these things become stronger as they behave on a daily basis. And the nature of every person is a virtue and natural that if you try to act in parallel with the person, the person is talking on his own, if he is worried about you, then the mind automatically touches that thing and you also have similar feelings about that person. And such feelings are increasing day by day, which means that this non-stop miracle also continues like this. The closed clock also shows real time twice a day. So if we are human beings, we know very simple but how to spend time.

Chapter -17 -Changing Strategy

A college symbol is what captivates everyone by showing off their craftsmanship during the period when everything is in a different order and unique period. Not only does it apply to the person but it also affects the person's behavior. And it is experienced by everyone but he is not aware of it. Everyone knows about cricketers. They are known by their names, their style of play and their blackness in a different field. By working hard day and night, they make a name for themselves and make a name for themselves so that their fans grow and their minds are drawn to them.

Fascinating, there comes a time when his style diminishes the show, after which he gradually reduces the impression of the mind and walks backwards. A lot of people are fascinated by their pre-election rhetoric and talk about how much will change, how much will change, and how many days after the election it will prove how much has changed. Are gone. Slogans are given through speeches that will develop the world by honestly working hard. And then when the child and that time comes, no one goes forward except to work for money. Then it took a couple of minutes for the wind to change, just like the seasons. Naturally, we have all learned that summer is just like winter season but it is not like that. The person has no place in his nature, his behavior, his living. No one looks back and forth to leave the parents in the old age home with the same stubbornness that they have always promised to serve their parents. It has no place. Sometimes I think everything is wrong but sometimes I think it is right. Before marriage, many people make thousands of promises that even when they do not have the strength to fulfill them, they are free to say whatever comes to their mind, then when the time comes, the soul is basically lost and when it comes time to fulfill it, they cannot fulfill it. It is unknown at this time what he will do after leaving the post. Wrong but there is nothing you can do about it but you can't change it. Because on the land on which we live, all these events in the life of every person are visited in some form or another on a daily basis.

If there is any information in this world, there are many institutes which require a lot of concepts for the happiness of the students and also for the help of the poor. What they don't even know is that by doing so, they too resort to corruption and make their institution's name white.

And basically when a person opposes it and tries to go a good way, for some reason or another, that person is either saved or his name is erased from this world. And the good news about the man who killed him in two days is that even the simplest of people doesn't have a simple shock to his name, and no one can stop those policies about the world being like this. It often happens in academic life that even though we do not understand every teacher well, many people treat them well if they pass school or school with the idea of treating them well and speaking politely, then there comes a time when they do not even have time to look at them. Because everyone in this world lives for the same thing, that is, the world that happened to be better for oneself, we forget the last Guru, because the law of creation is the same, when one's own work is done, no one has to take anyone. One often wonders, what is wrong with us? So the answer is that no one is at fault. Even though these changes that happen to you are uncomfortably painful, they are just as valuable, so you may have to go ahead and smile at the person you met at this very moment in your life. That person will not be found again. I was in this moment, so there is nothing you can do about spending time thinking about who wrote what and who will go. When a rich man is surrounded by people and the respect he gets is even more valuable because his condition makes him known by four people more because of his area and which makes him a different identity in the society but sometimes it happens that the man whose condition is changed by money Comes and goes and then slowly people get a glimpse of their point of view but the more affluent person I was first assuring was suddenly reduced somewhere. But money is the name of the person. The nature of a person is education. The education of a person shows him the way forward from the point of view of his thinking. It can also change a person's respect by changing the policy. When a person who fails in school suddenly gets a good reward by passing an exam or when he is honored or honored in a big way by giving a big prize or in a big event then suddenly the person names him. That person suddenly goes as his friend, which means it's a miracle that the same people who get hurt when they are named can't even mention his name. In the end, the answer is no, because there is no end to those policies, because it is a never-ending miracle that will always happen naturally.

Your life is made up like a candle. When a new candle is lit after it has been lit, it burns with a very fast and attractive radiant heat. And with extreme intensity, her impression looks a bit different. But as the duration increases, the intensity and width of the candle gradually decreases. Because the intensity of the candle teaches us a lot. That the intensity of man also decreases with time. If it does not contribute to the breadth of its life in all its systematic ways, then its intensity also looks attractive when it is new, and its width decreases as time goes on. So it is equally important to keep yourself attracted and energized step by step. So that its width is not reduced. Basically, when a student passes with very good marks in school life, then after coming to the university, her marks are very low. It is the changing policy that tells you that if you are failing the way you are going, then why not change the way you are going to get? Because the guidance that a person needs is only and only through experience that his Guru has more experience than you. Following in the footsteps of the Guru is not wrong at all.

But what happens is that when you follow in their footsteps, you ignore those mistakes and it happens to you. You don't want to change policies. Because unless you understand that you are your own adversary or another, you cannot understand the nature of life because of this. And the biggest truth in the world is that in the next few years, you'll laugh at the mistakes you've made. Because the energy that was given to us by grief at that time, the energy will run at such a low rate in the future that you will not be harmed by his feelings. Each person's mind adopts a slightly different strategy. It's as if some people react when they hear it, some people keep it in their minds. It all depends on your experience and the changing strategy you have. When a tragedy strikes, we declare the outcome of our own life when our day is bad. But we ignore the 365 days of the year. Many people do not try to understand that the definition of life is inevitable if one person defines his life. Because the person in front of you has done it or you have done it, because you have the courage to write history in your hands. When we address every person to live every moment, he does not live without declaring that moment to be the last, if that life becomes sad or very happy in the mood of living every moment. And when the time comes for him to face failure, he always remembers that failure and leaves himself behind. When a person says something, he makes a box in his head and always remembers it when he actually sees it, and he never thinks hard. One thing to keep in mind with this policy is that if the person in front is hitting you with stones (words), instead of throwing the stones at them again, you should collect the stone and create a state of your own and enjoy the stones in Italy at its rate. Because now science and we have introduced so many new things that many things are made from waste that we can always enjoy. And in order to have such enjoyment, people are in dire need of the words that they use against people. Because along with unemployment, the number of these people is also increasing day by day. If a watchman beats a poor boy, and after a few years he stubbornly studies the boy and goes to a higher position, we see the peon saluting him with his hand rather than beating him. From this small example, one would think that the bodyguard who was beaten by the watchman also hit his body; But the blow hit him hard, which is why he started studying so hard that he wanted to see to this day what position the qualifications of the front depend on. One thing is clear from this, how difficult it is to change policy. But that would have been difficult if not more difficult. So it was even harder. But the word difficult seems to suit those people who never try in life. The word "difficult" in this world is made up of such a mixture. And even more so when we dedicate our eyes to the struggle of man with the stubborn alloy. It was as if the difficult word, after the battle, was over, that he had never been born. Our life is like a circus elephant whose life is forced to do new things every day. And no one learns this before he comes into the world, he has to learn what he has, no one earns sin and virtue before he lives. All those rites take place in this universe. In fact, these are the few days of man, every day he declares himself dead. But he forgets the world. Even with the knowledge that everyone wants to go to this universe one day or another. And whatever you want to do in this life, no matter how much money someone earns, everything will go down. But this does not mean that we should turn our backs on hard work in this world. Everybody will read your lessons one day or another when you ask people who are praising their success for their experiences. So not only can you take that guidance but you also have to fight the battle with sword in hand. And every person's experience in this world and his strategy, his patience is going to change at every moment through a total shape of life. Because the changing strategy in the creation is also an equally important factor that comes before the eyes of every person every day.

Man's policy never changes by saying this. It changes over time, naturally. There is no place for anything. Anyone can like anything at any time. And it can hate him at any time. Sometimes she can even assert her own right to that. And sometimes they can throw it away without telling you. So there is no need to expect too much from any point of view. Because, a person's creation, a vision of man can change at any moment. Every person has that style hidden in a different way. Which person lives in that hope till the end of life. So no one immediately takes it out of his head and even brings it to his mind. Exactly why this is happening has not yet been proven. But the symptoms of some things can also be noticed. For example, if someone comes in your friend's life with a better person than you, then your price is lower somewhere and that price sometimes changes so much that he does not even have to worry about his feelings. But if you love him with all your heart and know that you love him with all your heart and remember him as a brother, then you must believe that no one can take your place in his life. Sometimes it happens that we always depend on the person, we lighten our mind with the things he wants. It seems that there is no world in our life without this person. But over time, that is likely to change. And in any form when you go up, and the person who understands your world, the person is always in the same place where he was before. The intensity about him decreases. Because we consider him to be more influential than himself, his dignity is diminished somewhere. It's as if we can get a bigger world than this. And for any person when you are readily available. So the price you want doesn't stay the same. So why should man never lose his self-esteem in this changing policy. Many people find such a person in their life one day but they do not stay without talking. But for some reason, when a person's next journey is a different one. So somewhere that relationship seems to have diminished automatically. And does not react with the same enthusiasm. This is called in modern scientific language, we no longer have the same contact as before. Apparently, they could not stay away from each other even for a day. Such relationships diminish over time in different ways. But even when there is no such thing as anger or hatred behind this reduction, the threads of the relationship are automatically reduced. And they only talk about what they've been up to lately, or what they've been up to. There is a miracle in this gentle relationship. Which may have been experienced by many. If a person meets each other after many years and does not treat them as enthusiastically as they should, and even if someone has just made a simple joke, they put aside that meeting and take the quarrel to heart. And it has happened so many times in this world that it may not have happened with the person in front of it. And every person in life should keep in mind that when a person meets you suddenly after going too far, he will try to talk to you as kindly as you can, even when the relationship is not as strong as it should be. This shows that changing policy is not a man-made society. The policy is constantly changing. Some people's policies are very effective while some people's policies are just as effective. What matters is not how you

start your life but how you end it. And
everything has a beginning as well as an end.
And the end is more important than the
beginning. Because the beginning never
announces the result but the end and I come
with the result and you want to see the world,
not your beginning and your hard work. Every
teacher has a dream that his student should be
in front of this life. But one thing no one knows
is that in this world, if there is a difference
between the teacher and the student, then the
student is more grateful. Don't know what is
behind his selfishness? As a child, many
teachers get angry and even beat their students
for not understanding a thing once. But now
there is no point in annoying the students. And
some students at that time have a different
struggle of education and at the same time of
teacher. It seems that the teacher is the best
person. But day by day, when he leaves school
and sets foot in university, he begins to feel that
the same teacher is small. So what if you say no
to a policy that changes this policy? No one can
say the reason behind this. Can only share in

the heart of the mind. The kind of hatred behind it is completely absent. But some elements of ego make a big difference in that policy. There is no need to create any kind of inferiority complex in the mind because there is no one in this world who has kept these things with him from the beginning till the end. And that is not at all the same zeal with which they started. There is not a single person in this world who has completed the beginning with the same path, with the same people, with the same 100% feeling till the end. Because is always starting in one way, in order to sustain it, both ways have to be built with such a strong vision. Maintaining a relationship is one of the most difficult tasks in the world, and it is very difficult to make sure that the person in front of you is just as enthusiastic if you are ready for it. And there is no one like him who has managed to survive in this world. There comes a time when man loves to be alone. When she is alone, she can make changes according to her own mind. She does not have time to wait for anyone to change. There is no time to expect from anyone. And the most important thing is that no action can be taken that will offend one's own mind. It is safe to say that this is not the case. It starts to feel like a big area. If the mind does not want to share any kind of difficult decision. The simplest answer is to understand the rules of life. That is, there is a reason behind what is happening in this world that ordinary people do not see. Every person's life is also different and it is made through different. The ups and downs of their moment is very different and rare. So there is no need to differentiate and understand your policy with each person. What is happening is happening right. If you win, you are succeeding and if you are losing, you are learning something from it. Because the policy that we took yesterday has changed today and will change again tomorrow. Because it is inevitable that things will continue to change in this world. And everyone wants everything in this world to be neat and tidy. But he does not think at all that today we should try to change ourselves every morning with a new change that will come in the work of other people. No one thinks so, and those who think so have made history. Because along with the changing pylons, they had also changed their manners in a way that would help them in the next few days. Singing the praises of the elders is a good thing but very few people think about the changes they have made in their lives by which their virtues are in our village.

Because everything has a definite duration. Until his day, those things start to feel very good, but there comes a time when man starts to dislike them. Which he can never tell to any person by word. It is not possible to find happiness in everything, but even if we try to act with the understanding that there is no harm in that, if we wait for its change, the wait will soon be over. Sometimes due to changing policies, when the wrong moment in life comes in a person's life, who is the most important moment to deal with? You don't even try to make a change unless something hurts you. The rules of the world are bound to change, but if you immerse yourself in them, you will not be harmed by the changing policies. One thing that was learned from the study of human physicians was that it takes 21 days to learn anything new. Because doing the same thing over and over again for twenty-one days can cause problems somewhere. But after the 22nd and 23rd days, man feels as comfortable as he is breathing. But the important thing is what day you are trying to change. Some people try to make changes in their minds but they are not happy about it. When you act naturally, there is a different kind of enthusiasm. Otherwise, when you say that you are forced to do some work, you will not be bothered by that problem and you will never have the interest to do that work. If you try to complete every task with joy, if you do any task with love, then hard work becomes as easy as playing a pinch. If the mind stays in one place and tries to work, it helps to make the work easier and more successful. When things are approved for you. That is, it takes a lot of patience and courage to convince the mind of what has happened outside of your mind. But in the changing policy, things will continue to go on like this, not everything will be to our liking. And the day you can readily accept things that you can never change, then understand that you are understanding the world. You can understand the world by thinking of many ideal thoughts, but you have no idea when those feelings will be shared with you. You already have a meal ready for any upcoming event. Then you never get in trouble. Because that thing is easy for you. If you want to be happy, understand your reaction from the heart, you want to move forward. So the whole thing can't be the same for you because of a changed thing. And so the stages in life will come. When you are ready to face the coming crisis, it seems that the price of the previous crisis was small. And last but not least, the headline made you read this article. That would be your price. And all of that reflects what kind of player you are A person who has passed away may come back if your luck is strong. He said that he also likes the name. But in all these times, time is so important that once it is gone,

it never comes back. And even the thing that
has to be regretted and repented, time never
comes back. But when we think of the past
when we go into the future, it seems like a
button was supposed to be made, when we
finger it, we can go back to that time and
improve our future there. And for some as a
baby gets older, he or she will outgrow this. But
it would be even better if he understood the
lessons of his life without talking it for granted.
And no one learns without making mistakes.
Because man's needs are such that they can
never be fulfilled in his life. Like changing policy,
his needs also change from time to time. Stress
is also changing so much that he is so engrossed
in correcting his stress that he forgets to live life
on his own. These are just some of the goal
setting shareware that you can use. Whoever
eats it then has real fun. Once that time is gone
you will never be able to enjoy it. The taste of
ice cream is a different kind of fun. It's a
different kind of juice. The tongue never
remembers the taste of life again. Because
eating ice cream over time is like thinking about

a change of policy. Some things are not expressed by this feeling. But we can understand it through their actions. There are moments in the lives of many people that they will never forget. But the thing that makes it happen is that it connects with our literal full life. If a person has seen a person close to him moving away from himself through a very tragic event, then that person has also moved away from this world. So its effect on the mind is so great that it literally changes. The person who is always smiling and joking literally falls in love. Because that person's smile has disappeared with this small incident.

Chapter 18- Natural change

Just as the fingers of a hand are made of different shapes, so it is human nature to be made up of different elements. His nature is shaped. Some people get so caught up in the nature of it that some people get confused about it for the rest of their lives.

In fact, there is nothing wrong with that. It is because of the way people look at each other that they are able to change themselves. There are very few people who express their inner feelings. In fact, it is very difficult to be natural. In this world, because which person will ever change, which person's behavior will change, what kind of person will ever develop? It has no place. Accordingly, it is important to make changes in your behavior from time to time. And the element of temperament is also unforgettable and so is the mysterious change. Because it is going to change. Most people have a passion. The root cause of this is the findings so far that if there is an atmosphere of tension in the home from an early age, then the nature of the child will formulate the policy accordingly. So the happier the atmosphere at home, the happier and happier the child will be. But any change in this depends on the situation of the person, if the atmosphere of stress at home is created automatically, then the person can do nothing about it. One can only try to choose a better way to live. But it has become very difficult in this time of inflation. To keep everyone calm and happy. Everyone likes to be happy but according to the situation that arises with him, he announces the policy in his nature. It all depends on the nature of the person. And the human instinct is so much better that it is often easier to understand the nature of the person in front of you after the first visit. With some people when happy things happen in a good and very good way. It is as if you are forgetting your grief because of the change that has taken place with it. Also, if a person is happy on the inside and something sad or angry happens to him at the same time, then his nature creates a different policy. If the thing is one percent, then the reaction is one hundred percent. Because it is difficult to understand why this miracle that does not work teaches a person. But basically if a person tries to be happy at any moment, he does not need a reason to be happy without worrying about anything. His mind can be happy and happy at any time, if he wants to. It doesn't take much effort. If you are fully motivated to move your emotions upwards, you can manually change your temperament. Not only does the nature of a person depend on his behavior and his will, but most people know the meaning of maturity. And maturity is the true sign that a person does not need age to develop maturity. Maturity also contributes a great deal to the experiences that come with it. And accordingly temperament also changes in a person. Some people do not believe in themselves because their nature often tries to lead them astray. Man never takes a wrong step with his own mind. His nature is often the reason for this. For example, if a person has a greedy nature, no matter how much he is given, he will never have peace of mind. And for the rest of their lives, such people are always on the lookout for more and more, but their never-ending miracles, such as selfishness and people, never stop. Some people's temperament is made up of "selfish" tendencies. In which they think so much of themselves that they have nothing to give or take from the other good or bad. But that doesn't work because once you see a person in trouble and try to make yourself better by leaving him or her alone, one day the miracle will happen that you will be in the place of that person's crisis. And these are just a few of the many instances where people have found themselves in a predicament one day. And this experience has come to many people step by step. And there are things that change the nature of the person who brings us the qualities that we assimilate. He assimilates certain types of elements in response to the coming circumstances and events. A lot of people think a lot of things in a calm state of mind. When he is in a state of skepticism and anger, he doesn't have the intelligence he wants and often the person's intelligence doesn't work in anger. It is also said that anger eats away at a person's intellect. And from the fact that there is complete agreement, the angry person does not know much about what he is talking about. When you **speaks** in anger, it often happens that he does not even know what to say to the person in front of him, so often it does not take long for even a small thing to become a big topic. And man's failure does not take him away from everything. He can lose his kingdom even in anger. For example, there are many people in history who would have written their names in gold letters in history, but there were some people who lost a lot of things in anger. And in today's world of everyday life, too, many people seem to have broken off their relationship in a fit of rage. The only thing that happens to them now is nothing but remorse. Just because a person doesn't like the other person doesn't mean he doesn't always try to like the person on the inside. Basically a person's temperament sometimes forces him to stay away from it. It is not at all possible for a person to become a scholar after coming into this world, forcing him to change his color according to the events that are to come. Most people also know that when we talk to a lot of people in a fit of rage, how they react to it shows how much potential they have. This does not mean that they do not feel bad about it at all. Anger and grief are the two things that have caused many people to end their own lives in the wrong way, so such incidents also lead to a change in temperament and are just as important. So the person needs to have patience and restraint on his feelings. It is also important to exercise restraint on your anger. Because it is very understandable that if a person speaks in anger, his words are no less than the sharp and deadly scripture of a sword. And it is also said that when a person speaks, he falls right there. And the common denominator from this is that when a person gets angry in life. So he accepts it when he has nothing in mind. It has also often been the case that one's anger is directed at one another and one's self is relieved. Sounds good enough for that, but it always seems boring to the person in front. Because the important thing is that there is emotion in the person in front but the person in front can also say a lot in anger. So it is very wrong to have such a disposition. Because when a person leaves, that feeling of remorse gives a different kind of trouble. Which is not even a thousand in the anger of the person in front. And all of this has an effect on her trust and understanding of each other. And there is no greater sin than committing any human emotion. The length of the temperament also cannot be measured like most things. It is also often unpredictable what kind of person behaves in the light of their temperament. Not only that, some people have a tendency to tell everyone exactly what they want to say without saying anything. The basic reason behind this is that they have created their nature and the value of their nature. In fact, a person's words are not so important, the way he behaves helps to explain his nature more than words. And the greatest truth in the world is that in nature, no matter how much a person lies, his eyes always tell the truth. Because in his eyes there is a purpose behind everything. The reason for the increase in rates is that the person inside the person is still small, if you look at the truth. But as he tries to grow up with thoughts, he still can't erase the perfection of his inner child as he wants. So how the eyes always tell the truth. The funny thing is that some people believe in words, but it is not always the case that the words they utter are based on the same words. Therefore, she will believe in words, but the nature of connecting and maintaining a relationship is not very long. And every person is made up of both good and bad things. Basically, his nature changes according to what happens to him. At times, she even thinks that the work we are doing is wrong, but if it makes her feel good, she will often feel that it is good. Every person is always good natured as a child and in his nature a kind of straight path is chosen. And as its sequence of events takes turns through different, its nature changes. For example, when a person is always reaching the pinnacle of success, there comes a time when a different kind of ego falls upon him. Emphasis on that ego changes our nature. And in this way, because of his ego, he always despises the person in front of him. In fact, he goes on such a diet, behind that ego that he forgets that there are more intelligent and successful people in this world. And what some people like about their nature is that they are always ready to participate in the success of any person and increase their self-confidence, and one thing about such people is so good that today or tomorrow their deeds always help them to move forward in life. And not only that, when a student or a person wants to be together in the face of adversity, he will never be alone in life. Because he is trying to earn good money through some means. But the thing is that there is a big difference between forcing oneself to be like that and staying natural with the help of human nature. In fact, man should be aware of all these things in his mind. One more element of such dispositions resides in the minds of all of us. Which is called "innocence." In the current era of 2022, it can be said that this nature is extremely dangerous during this year, even for those people who remain naive. I can say that this is not a world of innocence. In fact, more than half the world is surrounded by these people. And accordingly their numbers are increasing day by day but as long as they are not hit by anything, their nature never changes. And in fact, one more thing that has come before the world is that when a person expresses his thoughts and tears fall out of his eyes, then those people are the most naive. Such people should never do this because it would be a kind of sin. According to their demands, many people think that these people are fools. But the real reason for this is not how stupid it is. The real reason is that they think of everyone so they behave like that. They don't understand what kind of treatment you are getting. They are always confused. The real reason behind this is that they are considered as fools by the people, because they have paid their own price in front of such idiots

Would have spent. That's why they have to deal with such things. And the only thing left is why there is no need for such people in this world because it is time for them to deal with it step by step, and for that reason they suffer these losses. There are many instances where people are cheated and their hard earned money is snatched away from them in the age of internet. In fact, the rest of the people can do nothing but swear sympathy to such naive people. But extreme pity comes when it happens to those people. But people who don't even realize how much is wrong with them. The poor always show their faith in the person in front of them and they go that way. And there are two types of innocence. Some people are basically naive and some people pretend to be naive. Which people now do not recognize. People are pretending to be naive even when they know everything. Even when they are treated badly, when they meet in any moment of life, they behave as if they have been treated very carefully. A lot of people were also found in the tone of innocence speaking sweetly and condemning them from behind. In fact, the person who hurts you by speaking the truth on his face is better, while the person who comes in front of his mouth, after saying it, sweetens his mind by saying sweet words and he is the one who condemns you behind his back. But one of the best things that has happened in this world in the year 2022 is that nowadays, when a person criticizes another, people treat him only by recognizing his worthiness, because even through that, people understand his nature. It is the nature of many people that no one should leave them, so they climb any level. There are many examples of this too but before giving an example one thing is said that the motive behind it is also different. Some people have selfish motives behind it and some people have real affection for it. We request to stop any person but it is the nature of some people not only to make the request through different means but also to give us sometimes by looking at the level of request which person can request through which. Sometimes it feels wrong if you look at it personally, the policy behind each person requesting is different. But one thing to always keep in mind is that even if the person in front of you is not interested in staying with you even for one percent of what you have given, you are wasting your time and effort in such a place. But if there is a feeling inside you, it is that this person is not going to leave and he is not going to move away from you at all, he would have fallen in love with you. So every time you have to ask, when the time comes, you should also apologize because apologizing doesn't make anyone big or small. And one thing to believe is that the person who gave you that kind of love will never leave you, and what is more, the person I consider to be your best friend may be angry with you as much as possible but can never try to leave you. No, because no one is coming to take your place. Many people also call this nature "ribald". But this is not a quintessence, but a feeling of love in the heart, a feeling that always reminds us of the person in front of us. And you shouldn't feel bad about it at all, even if someone close to

you says two words to you in anger. Because by
staying together for so many days, they have
the same right over you and you also have the
same right over them. If there is no such right,
then the place to understand is not yours. But
some people also forget their self-esteem in this
tone. It often happens that it is important for
you to put your self-esteem behind you and
dance and match with the person but if the
person in front is not thinking accordingly then
he is really telling. Let's try to convince them
that these things are not possible. And you
should always try to move forward in your life.
Because not only have many people harmed
themselves through their temperament and
emotions, but they still think that at some point
they believe that the person who left them can
come, but when we see the person who leaves
and spends his life elsewhere, he is happy.
When they do, forget that they miss you too. If
the person in front of you can forget you so
easily but others don't mean that you didn't
have a small but love in your relationship. Even
so, owning one is still beyond the reach of the

average person. There is always an occasion in every person's life when a person leaves without any reason. What exactly is the reason behind this? They do not know until the end. Such behavior is often referred to as misunderstanding. It always happens that some people create a different wrong feeling in themselves due to small things which causes them to break off their relationship in the form of misunderstanding. A lot of people know that his nature is very wrong and he is not ready to admit even though he is wrong every moment. And the person who admits his own mistake means that he can do his best to change his nature. When one thinks through a certain process, one realizes that when a person tries to change his wrong nature, there is certainly a small degree of remorse in his past. Because so that the person does not try to change easily. Sometimes it is very difficult to make a change on your own, but it is also necessary to give a little trouble about what is happening today, but by going to tomorrow, the same trouble works to make your identity different and attractive. When a person is in pain because of something that is happening to him, his nature does not change, but in a way his nature calms down. And not only that, but his career has changed dramatically. And there are two aspects to each temperament, just as there are two aspects of the rupee coin. Both aspects are completely different from each other. The nature of some people is often difficult for people to understand but once understood people create a different kind of distance from that person. But man's condition often makes him spontaneous and compelled to act contrary to nature. And there has to be complete agreement because the person cannot always be natural because as much as the person can try to change the direction in which the application is being made, but by keeping himself completely clean he can do harm to himself. Not only this, with the help of good temper you can do wonders. How many times has it happened that when a person does not remember these two things name and face, then he is known by his nature and also by his

nature. And for some as a baby gets older, he
or she will outgrow this. Because temperament
is a kind of exercise. If your temperament is
good, then of course its benefits are on the
person in front of you and your opinion about it
automatically changes accordingly. For
example, when a person's temperament is very
sweet and humble, he always has a good feeling
in his mind about the person in front of him. It
is a very wrong thing for a person to never
forget which person will come to your aid and
even before helping, when a person is thinking,
he decides whether to help or not by looking at
his nature. And in those days, every person is
always thinking about himself, so he often
misunderstands the front and makes the logic
of his nature according to his own mind. For
example, a person may be talking to friends on
a daily basis, and for some reason, because a
friend is at work, when he reduces his speech
and speaks after many days, he argues that his
temperament has changed when the subject is
different. But in this world around 2000,
opinions about each person change from time

to time. If a person feels good about you, you respond by saying that the person has a very good temperament and that the person has a very good character. The reason behind this is because the person feels good about you and is always appreciated in your heart and in your words, no matter how bad he is. Basically, if you think about it, it can be said that this nature is very dangerous and not beneficial. Because a person with such a nature can never be anyone's friend. So you should always read from them. If a miracle is performed, a person of this nature is created on a large scale. So try to be with good people as much as possible so that we are ready to assimilate good things automatically. For example, when a student is lacking in study, but when he is with smart people in the team, then that change also happens in him. And the companionship that makes a person feel good should be maintained throughout their life. And because of these bad experiences you learn a lot of good things from it, just as nature has a similar role in our lives. That is, you can test each person on your own by nature. But before examining others, you must first be fully aware of your own nature. The person who comes running for help is definitely the one who brings life to you. If anything goes well, the slanderer is your opponent. And if you delete the birthday date of the poet wherever you are going through all the internet, your mother will be the first to wish you a happy birthday. Behind your good success are your well-wishers who support you. And this is not a one-day month. Depending on how you treat people throughout the year, the person in front of you has assimilated the nature of you. But the person who comes to your rescue should not be considered less than God. So in nature there is a different element hidden in each person which is definitely not stopping.

Chapter 19-A precious rule

First of all, just as there are some basic facts behind what individuals do before they start, there are also some important rules behind it, which most of the time have an important role to play in giving them a shape and a certain kind of twist. In fact, it is not at all the case that this rule is made only for mysterious changes. Gradually, when you practice it, you realize that certain rules have been made. Some people respect their own discipline by following those rules. So some people, those who follow those rules often go against them and make their own identity with a different vision. In fact, the rules are made so that the person has a purpose behind everything in a systematic way. But most of the time, people are always abusing it. Most of the time a person whose behavior seems artificial, wants to understand what rules you are trying to follow. Not only this, with the help of fire you can do welding. But you have to work hard to be a slave to the rules. Because the important rules are made by the administration itself, whether through any means or from any point of view. It could be that some of the approaches are wrong for us to look at and most of the time we are also against them. But if you are the only one who is opposed to it and the others are in favor of it, then maybe the rule is right somewhere. It takes time for you to understand the uniqueness of it. For example, traffic rules should always be followed. But today people don't even have two minutes to go, so they always break the signal and go ahead. But he does not think that you will survive even if you are late today, but because of your negligence, not a day goes by that you are alive. In fact, we are going to die once in a lifetime. But we are going to live a thousand times. But who has the time for this, everyone wants to do everything immediately but against the rules. In fact, many rules have been born in this emergency period of 2020. As a result, most people have stopped looking at many rules. In fact, they were doing their best. In fact, in that crisis, the whole world has found hope, the world has undergone certain kinds of changes, in fact, one of the most important means to prevent them is unity and secondly, it is very important that people follow discipline and rules. So that the crisis will be avoided soon. Unless a person finds himself in a predicament, he is not fully aware of the rules. Most of the 20 people say a lot about the importance of rules, obedience to the rules to guide them but many people ignore it. And so we give birth to many mysterious changes ourselves. There is no need at all for each person to replace the other. Even if everyone tries to change themselves, their efforts will save them a lot of trouble and give them a safe life.

Even after the practical change, there are many rules in the life of man, which are invaluable to him. In fact, he desperately needs to understand those things, and as he grows older, different rules are made that are made by nature for most of his future. Not only this, with the help of these rules, certain mysterious changes take place in their lives. Just as some natural laws pertain to our lives, their descriptions are often understood not only by words but also by a person's movements. Many idealistic people, when presenting some of the events related to their success, realize that the most important thing in their life is how well and thoroughly they understood the rules. As an important factor, you have to put it into practice. Because you have to follow the rules in time. There is a time when you want to move forward, but if you do not try to move forward in life, it means that somewhere you have forgotten your responsibilities, duties. This requires a great deal of adherence to important rules. The implication is that no one made this rule. Something like how different and precious each person's life is. And it's not even made in a certain way. And no one's life is the same. It is natural that the rules of each person's life will be different and invaluable. It depends on the person's perspective on how quickly he or she sees the rules and makes a mysterious change in his or her life. In fact, one of the important messages for this is to spend ten to fifteen minutes a day in life. In fact, a person who is honest with himself is less likely to make mistakes in the future because he knows himself so well. You can correct yourself by repeating the rules over and over again. In fact, as most people know, the hardest thing to do is to follow every rule. But if the rules are related to your life and your future, no matter how boring it may seem, if you are going to benefit from it in the future, then you should definitely try to follow the rules. There are also precious rules that can free you from future regrets. The most important rule for this is "patience." In patience is one of the most important rules in life that should be kept in mind. When it comes time to break up your relationship, the most important rule is "price." It is the price, not the item, that is the most important emotional gift to the person who lives your life. The value of the person is determined by the behavior you give them, but the rule is that when you try hard to maintain a relationship in front of the person, then the value is zero, then your efforts may be in vain. The rule again is that "decisions" are made in your life. Your decision is a very important factor in making mysterious changes. It is very important that you pay special attention to your decisions because of the rules. So why is every decision important? Because change will happen accordingly. And if you want change to your liking, you don't have to look at other people's rules. Life is yours, you want to make it happen in the future, not only that, but there is a mysterious change hidden somewhere in between. So creation has created a lot of things that we understand well, so we have to make our own rules and move forward in life accordingly.

Chapter 20- The last truth

If you look closely at your life, you will see one thing in every moment. And if you look closely, your life is like a season. Sometimes it rains, sometimes it rains, sometimes it covers winter to some extent. Not only that, but in the lives of many people, memories are also associated with the seasons. Which we express through emotion. In fact, this is what life is all about. If a person is trying to find happiness even in sorrow, then perhaps he has laid the foundation of it with a very strong vision. And for some as a baby gets older, he or she will outgrow this.

In fact, a person can never change the truth. What is going to happen is going to happen. In fact, if you are sad today, then maybe you should live in such a way that tomorrow will be a good day. Because only and only your day was bad not your life. In fact, things get happier when you look at the present and observe the events of the present and react to them. But nowadays, the damage that is going to be done is due to one's thinking. Thinking about things that haven't happened, planning ahead for things that will happen in the future that could change at any time. So there is a truth to everything. Most of the time, nothing can change that. I mean, I'm talking about mysterious changes. In fact, the soul within you, I try to do everything for you. But most of the time you get so caught up in it that you don't want to accept what you have to accept. Not only that, but most of the time the person rejects you equally. We always want the same person in our mind. If you think about it, if you assimilate and accept the person you want at such a time, then maybe your life will be much easier. But our mind never thinks about those things. Because it is probably a little difficult to bring about this mysterious change through emotion. And the biggest change comes when we learn to accept things. It is not so easy to accept everything as you like or without. One of your decisions can take your life, and it can end it. Most of the time your mind needs to be

taught a lot of things, and no one can teach it
except you. And most importantly, nothing in
this world is completely inhabited. There are
many reasons for this, not only if you find
something while living, but you are also
responsible for it. The fact is that no one needs
to try to understand things from the inside out
even when they are not so big. Not only this,
with the help of mutual education we also
create a big place in the lives of people who are
less educated and intelligent than most of us.
This is a very wrong thing to do because it also
causes some changes that we have to go
through. You just have to be more
discriminating with the help you render toward
other people. Which most of the time should
be expressed by true events. Much of this truth
is made up of a vision of change. Also, the
biggest factor in life is the coming and going of
the person. There are very few people who are
with you from beginning to end. But the
greatest power in life to bring about change is
to come and go. One such important last truth
is that when you think of some of the past

tensions in the district and the injuries caused by the feelings that have befallen you after you reach the future in life, most people smile. And often he even says in his mind, "How stupid I was to have all these things create stress." Because the whole game is about the intensity, the moment. Sir, if there is always a discussion about something that comes to mind every day, then the subject is chewed like this. It doesn't change most of the time and things change when it is forgotten. But the most important thing is what is being discussed. If there is a hot topic in the current situation, people will never forget it. For example, if you become an IS officer, people will forget in two days, but if you become an IAS officer, you will be caught in corruption. So people will remember you for a lifetime. And with all this, another important and final truth is that your biggest fan in this world will be someone you don't know. But the person who is most angry with you will be the one closest to you. But it is also the biggest truth in the world, that every person is becoming a real wanderer in someone's life. It cannot be changed. If everyone in this world is doing this to you, then understand that there is something wrong with you. Because it may not be completely impossible, but for a moment it can be said that you are a memory of someone's life. In fact, you are everything, not only that, you have everything, the question is also in you, the answer is also in you, the good things are in you but the bad things are in you. You have the strength to work hard, you have the strength to be lazy. But who wins in the end? This question, however, will fall on everyone. The simplest answer to the fair is what was their choice. And through their choices, this mysterious change has taken place. Not only happiness but also sorrow is in every person's life. Win is also in everyone's life and Khan is also in everyone's life. In fact, winning is never a gift of fate, but the choice of the person who wins. Not only this, with the help of happiness you can do great things. If he wants to be happy, he must first get permission from his mind. So whatever the situation, if he wants

to be happy, you can stay. And this is the truth
of the last mysterious change.